'THE SOU

My God, I am Thine;
What a comfort divine,
What a blessing to know that my Jesus is mine!
In the heavenly Lamb
Thrice happy I am,
And my heart it doth dance
At the sound of His Name

CHARLES WESLEY

'THE SOUND OF HIS NAME'

✳

The Autobiography of
BERNARD J. HONEYSETT

THE BANNER OF TRUTH TRUST
1995

THE BANNER OF TRUTH TRUST
3 Murrayfield Road, Edinburgh EH12 6EL
P.O. Box 621, Carlisle, Pennsylvania 17013, USA

❋

© Bernard J. Honeysett 1995
First Published 1995
ISBN 0 85151 677 7

❋

Typeset in 11^1/2/13pt Adobe Garamond
Printed and bound in Great Britain
by BPC Paperbacks Ltd
A member of
The British Printing Company Ltd

Contents

Illustrations

Foreword

I count it a very great privilege and pleasure to have been asked to write the Foreword to this book. My pleasure arises from the opportunity to pay tribute to Pastor Bernard Honeysett, whose friendship I have valued for over thirty years. Although he entered the Christian ministry later in life than most men do today, that ministry has proved to be significant not only in Tenterden but also far beyond as well. In addition he has given his energies to support and to encourage men who have sought to restore a more biblical Christianity than that which was prevalent in the first half of this century. The years through which he has served in the ministry have been testing times in this country, but throughout this period he has proved to be a man of conviction. Sussex men are noted for a certain firmness and that is to be seen in Mr Honeysett, but it is significant that he has also proved open to further light from Scripture and, at a time in life when many men's views have become fixed, proved ready to respond to the demands of truth at considerable personal cost.

I first came to know Mr Honeysett when he was pastor of Jireh Chapel, Tenterden, and immediately realised that although his roots were in a tradition of experimental Hyper-Calvinism that I knew so well, his preaching already showed signs of other influences. In this book he presents us with a moving account of the development of his doctrinal understanding until he reached a more biblical position, which was also closer to that of an earlier Nonconformity. His new convictions were strong, but he has never lost a love for his earlier associates with whom he has shared a passion for experiential Christianity. His appreciation of the hymns of Joseph Hart which emerges from these pages is testimony to this.

Mr Honeysett's friends value him as a conversationalist and a counsellor. They are now able to enjoy his company through the pages of this book. A younger generation and those who have not had the privilege of knowing him will find delight in reading the wisdom of a senior minister in the Church of God who draws on a rich experience of His goodness, and at the same time, is able to present us with many fascinating cameos both of Kent and Sussex life and of English Nonconformity.

ROBERT W. OLIVER
Bradford on Avon, January 1995

Preface

I have often been helped by the biographies of God's people of other times and some years ago, with the hope of their being of benefit to my family circle, I began to set down some record of my own life. I was not really writing with publication in view but wanted to leave a personal testimony to our great and gracious God. The pages then completed were left until more recent days. Now in my eighty-second year, I am not able to preach as once I did and, mindful of how the pen can also be a means of blessing, I took out the pages again and shared them with a few good friends. They encouraged me to think of a wider usefulness, an opinion shared by my publishers, and so I was able to add to the testimony and put it together in this final form. I have to thank, particularly, pastors Erroll Hulse and John Gosden, Dr Robert W. Oliver, and the editors of the Banner of Truth Trust with whom it has been a pleasure to work. My gratitude is also due to my niece, Mrs Anne Bishop, who kindly did all the original typing.

Last, but not least, I want to pay a tribute to my wife, Gwendoline, who has always supported me in my pastoral, preaching and writing ministry.

I hope these pages may remind Christians of the older generation that there is work for us all to do while life shall last. Above all, the ministry of prayer is a means of blessing which we cannot assess truly. I have to pray now about many things I used to take for granted. It is wonderful that we can take 'all to him'.

My prayer for these pages is that they may help a younger generation to know 'the sound of His Name' and do good to immortal souls when my dust lies under a coverlet of grass.

BERNARD J. HONEYSETT
January 1995

I

The Honeysetts of East Sussex

I n an old farmhouse in Sussex on 7 December 1912, the family doctor called down the stairs, 'A ploughboy for you, Joe'. That was the first announcement that the subject of these pages had entered this world, like all others, 'born in sin and shapen in iniquity'. I was the second child born to Joseph and Lydia Ann Honeysett. A daughter, Edith Esther, was then six years old; another son, Douglas Henry, was to follow less than a year later, and another daughter, Dorothy Ruth, six years after that. Thus our family, which has always been a happy and united one, was completed.

A few particulars of my ancestors may be of interest, as it throws light on the section of the church of Christ into which I was born, namely, 'The Gospel Standard Strict and Particular Baptist', to give it its full title.

My paternal grandfather, David Honeysett (1840–1925) had a daughter who died in infancy, and two sons, John and Joseph, there being two years' difference between their ages. My father was born on 14 April 1881 and his mother was buried the following Christmas day. I have heard him relate how after the funeral his father went down the road from his small farm in an isolated part of the country to see if he could find a woman to give some attention to his babies. Soon after, his parents took the younger boy, and he managed to care for the two-year-old, often having to tie him to the leg of the table while he attended to the farm. Both boys grew up and worked on their father's farm, never receiving any wages, as the custom was in those days, but both receiving the gift of a silver watch when they were fourteen years of age. The logic was that when their father died they would inherit what he had – and what they had helped him to obtain! They eventually owned their own farms and for many years farmed two adjacent farms, Cowden and Tilley Farm, East Sussex. They were certainly hard times.

My grandfather married again, but enjoyed only a few years of married life. He was a hard-working, God-fearing man. All his life he attended the small Strict and Particular Baptist chapel at Bodle Street, a village in Sussex, though he never made an open profession by baptism and membership. He was the eldest of eight children, all of whom, I believe, lived to be over eighty, and two over ninety years of age. I well remember my grandfather and particularly his funeral on 19 June 1925. All his brothers and sisters were present, and as was the custom, the coffin was carried on a Sussex waggon. The bearers wore white Sussex smocks (an everyday outer garment of white worn over the other clothes), which was a custom peculiar to the south of England. A smock owned and worn by my grandfather is an exhibit on permanent loan at Michelham Priory, near Hailsham, East Sussex.

It was a very hot day, and I well remember the dust made by the horses and waggon and the numerous landaus which followed as we slowly traversed the two miles from the farm to the chapel. There were no tarred by-roads in those days! I also had on my first pair of long trousers! I do not believe that any of my grandfather's brothers and sisters were converted, and so we grandchildren were pushed into the carriage with the conducting parson as they did not want to ride with him.

My paternal great-grandfather, also named David, began to farm in a very small way in the early part of the nineteenth century, first owning one cow which he tethered on the grass verge beside the road. Later, he rented a small farm and by hard work he came to live comfortably for those days. He and his wife kept all their money in the house and she was always the banker. I have heard my father say that if they ever needed any financial help, the old chap would say, 'You must go and see mother'. I believe they were both godly folk, being founder members and life-long attenders of the chapel at Bodle Street. They died within a day or two of each other in 1894, and were buried together.

I think it is unique that my great-grandfather was buried on the spot where he was born, and this was very closely involved in the history of Bodle Street chapel. It came about in this way. Early in the nineteenth century, a Mr Rainsford walked the twenty-five miles from Brighton to preach in a wheelwright's shop in the village. After a few visits, the congregation increased and he preached in the open air on what was called 'The Green'. The outcome was that a chapel (Ebenezer) was built on this spot in 1835. Through one of these early sermons preached by Rainsford, a young man who had come to ridicule was convicted of his sin and saved. When he fell seriously ill, it was his wish that he might be buried on the spot where he was 'born again' and this was granted. Part of the floor of the chapel, three seats from the back, was taken up and the young man was interred. For years my family occupied this pew, but no record or tablet has ever commemorated this interesting account of God's sovereign work.

During my great grandfather's lifetime the chapel purchased the cottage and garden adjoining for a graveyard. This happened to be the cottage where he was born, and so when it was demolished and the ground used for a graveyard, it came about that he was buried on the spot where he had entered the world.

I feel certain that many of my forebears will rise to eternal bliss from that sacred piece of ground on the great resurrection morn when the last trump shall awaken the whole of Adam's posterity to appear before their Creator and Judge. What solemn and surprising revelations will then be made, and how final the verdict as there will be no higher court of appeal! Surely we all need to pray the prayer of Robert Elliot:

> Prepare me, gracious God,
> To stand before Thy face;
> The Spirit must the work perform,
> For it is all of grace.
>
> In Christ's obedience clothe,
> And wash me in His blood;
> So shall I lift my head with joy
> Among the sons of God.

My maternal grandfather (whom I do not remember) farmed Bromham Farm in the Heathfield district, about ten miles north of Bodle Street. He attended the Gospel Standard Strict and Particular Baptist church at Broad Oak,

Heathfield. This chapel appears to have been built some years later to a similar plan to the chapel at Bodle Street.

The Broad Oak chapel was pastored for a lengthy period by a Mr George Mockford, whose son held the pastorate at the Strict Baptist chapel at Devizes, Wiltshire for many years. He lived well into his nineties and he and my mother were friends in the Sunday school. My grandfather Haffenden was married three times and had eight children, of which my mother (1880–1968) was the youngest. I believe that all my mother's brothers and sister were true believers, but her father was a very hard man, much involved in his business. Although he always attended worship on Sundays, I have heard my mother relate a solemn dream that she had after his death, in which she saw all her family in heaven, but her father was shut out. We need to examine ourselves and not be satisfied with a mere outward profession of religion. How true are the words of Joseph Hart:

> *True religion's more than notion,*
> *Something must be known and felt.*

My grandfather moved to Pear Tree Farm, Bodle Street, when my mother was about fourteen years of age. He worshipped at the chapel until his death but was interred in the burial ground at Broad Oak.

My great-grandfather on my mother's side was a founder member of the cause at Heathfield and as far as I know was a humble, gracious man. The only real link I have is that, as the eldest son of my family, I have inherited his grandfather clock, which still goes very well and stands in my hall. It is one of the early brass-faced models and has only one hand.

My father (1882–1967) was a humble, hard-working

soul, but a poor businessman. He would often tell a story which certainly confirmed the last statement. When he was a lad, a dealer called to see if there were any articles on the farm for disposal. There was a piece of harness which his father did not require, so he went to consult him. His father said, 'Try and get 2s.6d (12.5p), but if he will not give that, take 2s. (10p).' My father came out and said to the dealer, 'I am to ask you for 2s.6d, but if you will not give that, I am to take 2s.'!

My father met with two serious accidents, which no doubt affected him. The first was before he was married. He was riding a young horse when it threw him and, as he fell, one foot remained caught in the stirrup. The horse turned for home and dragged him down a steep hill. Fortunately, at the bottom his foot was released just opposite a cottage. The owner raised the alarm and my father was taken home, where he remained unconscious for two or three days. Later in life he was thrown from his market cart, hitting his head on the hard road. The doctor said it was his hard bowler hat that had saved him. Although he drove a horse and cart for many years, I never considered him to be a good driver. He tended to be too hasty with animals.

When my parents were married on 18 October 1905, my paternal grandfather rented the adjoining farm. My parents lived in the farmhouse and ran the farm for him. Father's wages were then 10s. (50p) per week and they let one room in the house to an old lady for 2s.6d (12.5p), making their total income 12s.6d (62.5p) per week! After some years, when they had three children, my mother said she could not manage. The death of her father had brought her a small legacy and so they came to rent a farm near the Dicker and began farming on their own. They were there for eighteen months and attended the Strict and Particular Baptist chapel at the Dicker, one of the largest of these chapels in the south of England.

An incident stands out in my memory from the period when we attended that chapel. One Sunday I was naughty during worship. My mother took me to the top of the burial ground where there were some trees, gave me a good thrashing, and immediately took me back into the service! It has always made me sympathetic towards children during worship if they are restless, although I have on occasions found it a little trying when they really compete with me in the pulpit.

My grandfather was very 'put out' when my parents left Tilley Farm and at once gave notice to the landlord, the Earl of Ashburnham, to relinquish the tenancy. Farms were not easily let in those days and so it remained vacant for eighteen months until my father was successful in applying to rent it. There he was to continue until 1960, a stay of fifty-five years, purchasing it after the First World War. My brother and I really took it over when our father was unable to continue.

At this juncture I should like to give readers a picture of what life was like in those early days before the advent of such marvels as aeroplanes and television. Maybe no generation has seen so many changes as mine. In that old farmhouse of Tilley Farm where I first saw the light of day, we did not even have mains water or indoor sanitation, still less electricity or a telephone.

There were thirteen rooms, which included a very large wash-house with a well fed with rain water from the roof, and another deep well for drinking water. Three people would stand at the brick sink, washing the clothes in large baths. One end of this room led into the pantry and the other into the bakehouse, which housed the great brick oven used for baking bread etc. From here you entered the spacious kitchen with its cooking range, which was lit several times weekly for culinary purposes. The sitting-room was in daily use by the family, whereas the drawing room was reserved for Sundays and special occasions like Christmas.

Monday was always wash-day and my job as a boy was to light the two coppers, the larger one for washing the clothes, the smaller for hot water. I remember one morning, when the larger one was alight, my favourite cat came rushing out in great alarm. She had gone to sleep the night before in the warm ashes! For one with nine lives, it is surprising that the only injury was singed whiskers!

On Tuesday the washing had to be folded and ironed. The irons were at one time heated in front of the fire, then in later years on the kitchen stove. There was mending to be done, buttons to sew on and socks to darn. Money was usually in short supply, so clothes had to last. They were passed down to the younger children. Mother made a lot of our clothes, even our suits when we were small boys.

Wednesday was market day, when Father would drive to Hailsham cattle market, about seven miles away. Some business was transacted, then the rest of the day was spent discussing current affairs with other farmers and acquaintances. My brother and I were sometimes invited to accompany him, but he normally took a local seedsman with him. This man abominated laziness and often gave his opinion of his generation to my father, 'Joe, it won't make any sense till they get back to *work*!' What would he say today, I wonder? In those days a carter would have to start at 5 a.m. to have his horses fed and groomed ready to go to the field at 7 a.m. He would work till 5 p.m., six days a week. On market days Father would purchase anything that Mother needed. Conversation was always very lively at supper time that day!

Butter was made on Thursday from cream skimmed from the milk during the week and then churned. The churn was a wooden barrel on a stand and was rotated by hand. It had a little glass window in the lid, so that you could see when the butter had 'come'. In cold weather, it took longer for the butter to form. Sometimes one might have to keep turning for an hour, and this could prove very tiring. Mother then put the butter on a wooden table called a butter worker. Once the butter milk was extracted, the butter had to be made up into half-pound 'pats', each with a pattern marked on top and wrapped in greaseproof paper, ready for sale.

Friday was the day when Father did his 'round' in Eastbourne, a round trip of about twenty-five miles with his horse and market cart; this took most of the day. He took produce like butter, eggs, rabbits and, in season, various fruits and vegetables grown by Mother in the garden. These were sold either to shops or (mostly) to private customers living in large houses.

We children always looked forward to Saturday, when food for the week was baked. Pride of place went to a large roast joint of meat for dinner. This had to last us for the rest of the week in the form of pies, etc.

Everything had to be tidied up, ready for the visiting preacher, who usually came on Saturday evening. This was also bath night for us children, so that we all looked our best for the Sabbath. In those early days we were bathed in a bath-tub – often, in cold weather, in front of the fire in the living room.

Besides these activities on particular days, there were the regular chores. Every day all the lamps had to be cleaned and refilled with oil and the candlesticks cleaned and renewed. We children were only allowed a candle to light us to bed. The adults had hand lamps, but these were considered too dangerous for us. A supply of logs and other wood had to be brought in and stacked in the chimney corner – a job allotted to my brother and me. Then there were the cats and dogs to feed and a routine round to make the beds, which were feather and so needed a good shaking daily to make them fresh and comfortable.

Sunday was the day our parents particularly looked forward to – the day of rest, but not quiet! We rose about the same time, for the cattle, horses and poultry needed feeding and the cows had to be milked 365 days a year. All work had to be completed, breakfast eaten and all of us in our Sunday best, ready to drive to chapel by 10 a.m. Services never lasted less than one-and-a-half hours, after which we would return home for a meal and again attend to the animals, but *no other work* would be done.

In summer, after tea, we were allowed to go for a long walk – but no flowers were to be picked! Otherwise, the evenings were spent singing or reading, sometimes with other friends from the chapel.

We would be what was rightly called a God-fearing family. Even those who were not converted had a deep reverence for God and very high moral standards. In those days most people would have been ashamed to be seen gardening on the Sabbath. Grace was always said before meals, and Father always read a chapter from the Bible and prayed before we went to bed. It was rather formal and we were never actively involved. Father, who was very different from Mother, conducted his Sunday school class in the same way. After the opening, we went to our classes, and if we were in Father's, we just kept reading round from some part of Scripture, each boy in turn reading a verse, with no comment or instruction. Sadly, as scholars we simply counted to the next verse we were to read, placed one finger firmly on it, just relaxed and looked around! My dear Father, although a kind and gracious man, was rather narrow in his outlook and could be critical of other Christians outside his little group of churches.

When my Father was converted is not very clear, but it would seem to have been in his late teens. He recorded it in this way. On Anniversary Day at the chapel, when two services were held on a weekday, many folk would drive in their various horse-drawn vehicles and someone had to tend the animals during the services. This, Father was pleased to do until a year when the felt needs of his own soul led him to want to attend the services and hear the preaching himself. He was baptised on Christmas Day 1910 and remained an honourable member of Ebenezer Strict and Particular Baptist church, Bodle Street for fifty-seven years. At one time, he played the organ and started the singing, and for forty-three years he fulfilled the office of deacon, announcing the hymns as the custom was.

My father was a man of many fears and I have often thought that the couplet by Joseph Hart seemed to sum up his experience:

Make us well our vileness know,
Keep us very, very low.

His one great delight was reading hymns and the lives of hymn writers and other saints. He knew many of the hymns in Gadsby's selection by heart and could give you the number if you quoted a verse and usually tell you who wrote it too. He considered that for grandeur of language, there was no-one to equal Isaac Watts; for depth of experience, Joseph Hart; for hymns on the covenant, John Kent; for quaintness of language, John Berridge. Hymns with the sweetest spirit were those of John Newton; or if you wanted to be lifted to heaven, you should read Samuel Medley; he also highly esteemed the hymns of John Wesley, John Cennick, William Cowper, Augustus Toplady and, of course, Anne Steele. It was rather remarkable that the only hymn that he quoted on his death bed was 'The sands of time are sinking', a hymn not in his beloved *Gadsby's Hymn Book*. He passed to his eternal rest on 27 November 1967, aged eighty-six. My mother outlived him by one year.

Today, my elder son, David, and his family attend the chapel at Bodle Street, making six generations worshipping through the years since 1835.

My mother, who was of Huguenot ancestry, attended Broad Oak Chapel as a child, and it appears that God began a work of grace in her heart as a small child, for she remembered the conviction and the need which she felt then as the pastor quoted the couplet:

> *If the Lord should come tonight,*
> *Would my light be burning bright?*

After her father moved to Pear Tree Farm, she attended the chapel with her family. Her father married for a third time and her stepmother proved to be a very hard and unkind woman. I remember her quite well. She had treated my mother very harshly. On one occasion it reached the point of my mother determining to leave home, but when she was washing the dairy floor God applied the Scripture with power to her soul: 'I am the Lord thy God that teacheth thee to profit'. She said, 'That morning I washed the floor with my tears as well as with the water from the pail'. From then on she was able to bear her lot until she married and left home. It can be said in her honour that when her stepmother became old and lonely, she often visited her.

When thirty years of age mother contracted diphtheria and was so ill that doctors despaired of her life. It was then that God spoke to her in the language of Psalm 91:16, 'With long life will I satisfy him and show him my salvation', and she lived on for nearly another sixty years. She was baptised on 22 June 1922 and remained an honourable member for fifty-eight years. She was a very discerning listener and living through much tribulation required strong meat in the preaching. I remember one preacher who often said, 'perhaps', 'maybe', 'I hope', etc. and my mother's comment was, 'I want more than that; I must know and be assured'.

My mother was an excellent businesswoman and we all owed a great deal to her efficient management. For many years through the dreadful depression of the 1930s she worked very hard, taking in paying guests in the large farmhouse, keeping all the accounts, doing most of the business and taking produce into the town once a week. Many were the occasions when we had to wait on the Lord to provide for us, and many were the wonderful answers to prayer.

One incident I record which shows the faith with which God blessed her. We needed a new car and she had heard of a second-hand one, which on inspection she agreed to purchase for £30 and to collect and pay for at the end of the week, but without having a penny towards what was, at that time, a large amount. Saturday dawned and she was still without the money. During the morning someone called at the farm to see if a certain large henhouse was for sale. Mother replied, 'Yes, I want £30 for it'. The person agreed, paid the price and mother went off to collect the car and pay as promised, doubtless with a heart filled with praise and thanksgiving to her heavenly Father for hearing her prayers and granting her request.

For many years we entertained the visiting preachers each Sunday and I believe my mother often encouraged them and on occasion voiced her disapproval if she felt they had failed to do justice to their subject. Like all Christians, she had her weak moments, and I remember her being tempted to buy a ticket for a sweepstake and the dreadful anxiety she felt lest she should win and all the world know of her sin.

She was an excellent letter writer, and I have a box of her letters mainly written to her closest friend whom she met on her honeymoon, and with whom she corresponded for the remainder of her life. She was also very attached to her sister, Lucy, who had a gift for poetry and often replied in verse.

My mother suffered for many years from arthritis and was seldom free from pain. When seventy, the words seemed to follow her for over a month, 'There is yet much land to possess'. Another eighteen years were to follow, during most of which she was a semi-invalid from two very serious thromboses, spending many months in hospital. Yet she saw both her sons and younger daughter married and both sons and their wives baptised. The elder son (myself) entered the ministry and became settled in a pastoral charge and the younger became a deacon of the home church. After many pastorless years she saw a minister called and inducted and some building up once more of the little church so dear to her heart.

Mother passed to glory on 5 December 1968, the day after her eighty-eighth birthday. Just a few days before, with almost the whole family around her, she rejoiced in the full assurance of faith saying, 'I never thought I should feel like this. Why does not my dear Saviour come and take me to Himself?' Every fear was gone and her one great longing was to be with her Lord in heaven – a wish so soon to be granted. At such a time we can only sing, 'What must it be like to be there?' So both my parents came to their end 'as a shock of corn fully ripe'. My earnest prayer is that it may be so with my loved ones, and indeed with all who may read these pages. There is no other way to salvation but by saving faith in the Lord Jesus Christ. How true it is that 'there is no other name under heaven given among men whereby we must be saved' (*Acts* 4:12). 'Ye must be born again'.

My mother often told me what a sick and miserable little infant I was, but through the mercy and goodness of God and her care, I grew a strong and healthy lad and have enjoyed remarkably good health all my life. When I was five years old and my brother four, my sister went on holiday and contracted whooping cough, which in those days was very serious for young children. So rather than risk our catching it, we were sent off to a private boarding school in Heathfield, where we remained for our entire education, some ten years.

It was early in my school days that a deep impression of God was made upon me. I was taught to say a prayer when I went to bed and from birth had been taken to worship twice on Sundays. At school, the headmistress used to give us music lessons, which she would fit in at odd times. She had a violent temper and we were all afraid of her. One day I was sent for to have my lesson, but I could not find my music anywhere and in desperation I closed my eyes and asked God to find it for me. When I opened my eyes I saw it lying on the floor beside me! This was the first answer to prayer that I can remember and it had the effect of causing me to pray to God for help in many ways during my school days and later. I was not very brilliant at school as far as I can remember, and have always had spelling difficulties. Often I had to stay in and write out fifty or one hundred lines, a common punishment in those days and a very good one.

There is one other incident which stands out in my memory and which I record to my shame. On this occasion someone had done something wrong but when questioned none of us owned up. The teacher said, 'I know it is not Bernard because he always tells the truth'. In actual fact I was guilty and the fact that I got away with it caused me far more sorrow and distress than if I had confessed and been punished.

The discipline at the school was very strict and the food very plain. We seldom had a fire or much heat in the rooms, yet kept remarkably fit. We always went for a long walk every day, especially Wednesdays, which was our half day, when we might walk to Mayfield and back, a distance of eight to ten miles. The bread was always two or three days old and if we thought we were getting near the time for new bread, we would eat extra! For breakfast and tea we just had bread and 'marg' (without restriction but only one piece with jam or treacle), never any cake and only porridge made with water and a dash of milk. If ever we were invited out to tea, the next morning we all had a cup of senna tea for breakfast – an excellent purgative to expel any harm from the rich food eaten overnight! What a difference today over sixty years later. I often think of those days when I attend ministers' conferences in the various universities with their excellent accommodation and food.

One of the events of the year was the taking of examinations, which were set by the College of Preceptors and for which we had to travel to Brighton for four days. We were given fish, which was supposed to assist our brains, and allowed to go out to a restaurant for our midday meal and choose which dish we liked.

When we were old enough we each had a bicycle and went home for weekends – a distance of about ten miles. Before that we used to leave at 6.30 a.m. on Monday mornings, walk three-and-a-half miles, catch a bus from Herstmonceux to Hailsham, a distance of four-and-a-half miles and then take a train to Heathfield. My great love was gardening and horticulture rather than academic studies and I could hardly wait for my last term at school, which came in 1926.

A wonderful preservation belongs to this period which I must record. In the wash-house there was a large wooden pump in front of a deep well with an iron cover. The year 1921 was one of severe drought. That summer the water fell below the pumping line and water could only be obtained by letting a pail down on a long rope. One day, as my father had just drawn up a bucket and was setting it down, I ran out from another room and round the back of the pump, stepping into the open well. As I fell, my small fingers caught on to the tiny ledge, not more than half an inch deep, into which the cover fixed, so enabling me to be pulled out. Had I not been pulled out, I would have gone to a watery grave in my ninth year.

What a wonderful word is that, 'Are they not all ministering spirits, sent forth to minister for them who shall be heirs of salvation?'

Even before our conversion, God sends His angels to take care of us, evidence that we were chosen in Him before the foundation of the world. How we should ascribe all the glory and honour to God alone. 'By grace are ye saved through faith; and that not of yourselves: it is the gift of God: not of works lest any man should boast' (*Eph.* 2:8, 9).

So the first chapter in my life closed as I left school only to witness far more of the mercy, guidance and instruction which God purposed to unfold to me.

> *The fictious power of chance*
> *And fortunes I defy;*
> *My life's minutest circumstance*
> *Is subject to His eye.*
>
> *O might I doubt no more,*
> *But in His wisdom rest;*
> *Whose wisdom, love and truth and power,*
> *Engage to make me blest!*

2

An Old-World Country Chapel

I have already related how Ebenezer chapel, Bodle
Street, Sussex came into being. In this chapter I want
to give a picture of what worship was like there
and elsewhere and some of the experiences of people I
remember, or heard of from my parents.

The musical side of worship was led in various ways.
Sometimes it was led by a flute or small harmonium; in a
few chapels two or three instruments – violin, flute, etc. –
were used, but in quite a few the singing was often unaccompanied, the key note being sounded with a tuning
fork. Unaccompanied singing was usually slow, all parts
being sung, resulting in a good harmony. The hymns and
tunes were chosen by the deacon when the service was in
progress, during the prayer and sermon, and these would be
passed back to the various singers – a practice I always felt
was not very conducive to attention to either the prayer or
the preaching!

I remember two of the old men for whom my father had
a great regard, Mr Clarke and Mr Morley, both of whom
wore Sussex smocks. Unhappily, Mr Morley became nearly
blind; I remember hearing that one Sunday afternoon,
when there was to be a baptismal service, he walked down

the aisle, and not seeing the baptistry, stepped into it, standing with his smock floating on the water around him like an umbrella!

The Sunday services were at 10.30 a.m. and 2 p.m., and always lasted one-and-a-half-hours, as I have said. Three hymns were sung; if they were long the first verse was often omitted. There was a Scripture reading, a long prayer and a sermon usually forty-five to fifty minutes in length. Our dinner we normally ate in the chapel, cups of tea being provided, for which we paid a copper or two. There would be grace before the meal. I remember we did not like some of the men, because they went on praying too long, and we were hungry. We always had the same menu – a sausage roll, a jam tart, a scone, sometimes finishing off with a bun, all homemade of course. The reason for the times of the services was that almost all present would be farmers or farm workers, so they tended their stock and horses before coming, then went home to do the same before darkness fell. I never minded getting up and doing the rounds in the morning, but I always hated having to come back home, change my clothes and get back to the jobs of feeding, milking, etc.

On anniversary days, two services were held on a week-day with a tea in between. There were people who came to these services who did not attend on Sundays. I remember one man who attended saying that you could not get such a good tea anywhere for sixpence! There were still those who only came for the 'loaves and fishes'. The chapel would be full on such an occasion, but I fear there was a good deal of religious gossip, as well as some spiritual conversation!

Among some of the worshippers I remember as a boy were Mr and Mrs Edwin Wood, who walked about three miles; he had mutton-chop whiskers, and she had a very shrill voice. Mr and Mrs Isaac Message were another couple. He was a very quiet man, a deacon, although he never engaged in public prayer. They walked a great distance and were always there early to light the tortoise-slow combustion stove which was the means of heating the chapel. Sometimes the wind blew in the wrong direction, or it was very damp and the stove would fill the place with smoke! This made it very cold and unpleasant, but by dinner-time, when we all clustered round, it would sometimes be nearly red hot, and we had to move back!

There was Mr and Mrs Will Meopham and their two sons who were farmers and only attended in the afternoon, as did the Fairall family.

On the first Sunday in the month when we held communion, some would come from other causes where there was no church membership and the Lord's Supper was never celebrated. On these occasions we would see Mr Daniel Cornford from Dallington, a farmer of Great Sprays Farm who always drove a light cart; standing very upright and with a dark beard, he sang alto in a falsetto voice. A sister from Ninfield, Nellie, one of two maiden sisters, also came; her sister, Hetty, was a member at Hastings, so rarely came. Nellie Mitchell was a very regular and gracious soul, and these two largely ran the cause at Ninfield, engaging the ministers and caring for the building etc. Their mother, who was a rough diamond, used to say concerning the chapel at Ninfield, 'Nell and Het fry most of the fish up there!'

Then there was Jesse Buss, a big man, and his wife Sophie, who was very tall and slim. He was a carrier, taking produce to town for various people and doing a big business in eggs. He was very sensitive. One day when someone was sitting in his seat, he said he thought it was the thin end of the wedge to get him to leave the chapel! Another old couple were named Hoad; when asked how he was in health, he always replied, 'Among the middlings'. A Mr and Mrs F. Styles moved from Kent to a farm about a mile from the chapel; she was a member at a Kent church, but he was not accepted for membership. Because of Isaac Message's unwillingness to speak in public, Mr Styles was asked to invite the ministers and announce the hymns. He had a large stool made and covered it with carpet, on which he stood to give out the hymns. My father was quite furious, saying it was the very height of pride!

There were many others, but what shall I say more for time would fail me? People thought nothing of walking many miles in those days. In the winter time, my father would sometimes walk to Dallington to an evening service when one of his favourite ministers, a Mr Fred Kirby, was preaching. He always preached with his eyes closed and spoke very rapidly, but with good pronunciation. At one time, we had a godly maiden lady living with us to help my mother; she would also go quite on her own along the country lanes on dark winter nights to Dallington, which must have been a round walk of eight miles, and that after a day's work!

I remember that after the church was much reduced there followed a season of blessing when there would be seventy to eighty in attendance on a Sunday afternoon; it then again declined, like so many other churches. This has often been the experience at Bodle Street chapel in the 160 years of its history. There have been five pastorates, some extending over a number of years. One minister, a Mr

Davies, commenced his pastorate on 1 January and died before the end of the month. I remember this sad dispensation of God, and how the little church felt deeply grieved.

I must mention a few of the ministers. In doing so I do not want to give the wrong impression; they were godly men, and a few were able preachers, but most were very poor, with no training or education. I wonder if some were really called to the office; perhaps they came within the 'helps' of Scripture? For many years we were without a pastor and the pulpit was filled with what were termed 'supplies' – men with a secular calling who travelled about preaching on Sundays. They mostly came on Saturday afternoon by public transport.

Joe Burt was a bricklayer from Croydon. He was a very big man with a huge moustache, who was very fond of singing. So after tea he would say, 'Shall we have a tune?' My elder sister, who taught the piano, accompanied our singing on our small harmonium. He used to sing tenor and would drag the notes terribly. When we had finished a hymn to a favourite tune he would say, 'Isn't that beautiful!' I remember little about his preaching.

Mr Manktelow was a coachman, a slightly built man with a pinched face. He used to address the Sunday school between the services. I remember him telling us one thing to illustrate the Scripture, 'Be sure your sins will find you out'. He said that when going round the village with a gang of boys, they thought it would be great fun to strip off some dock seeds and throw them over the garden of a cottage, something which they accomplished quite thoroughly. A few years later, his father moved into that same cottage and he was given the job of digging up the docks which had by now become large, deep-rooted plants!

William Pounds came to preach about once or twice a year, and was pastor of a church in Streatham, London. His father had held a pastorate at Bexley, and he was distantly related to my mother. Some of the older folk did not get on with his ministry; it was not experimental enough for them and they called it 'letter preaching'. But I always felt I had understood and gained some instruction, which was more than I could say for some of the others.

Then there was Jimmy Pearce (Sunny Jim). We children loved him coming because he had lots of tales to tell us. He was the pastor at Lee Common, Buckinghamshire and had been a very wild character before his conversion. Just one story will suffice. He told of a minister going to a revivalist meeting. Their cart broke down, which made them very late, but he said, 'Never mind, we got there in time to save ten!' How many might they have saved if they had been on time! We knew nothing of such meetings and it all sounded very exciting.

Louis Murrell was another 'help'; his sermons were mostly quotes from hymns, with something of his own experience. We knew when he was about to finish because he would say, 'May you . . .', 'May I . . .', etc. – which was his application. He came from a London church, and his pastor used to preach for us once a year. I remember this London pastor telling us of one of his members who was always very long in public prayer; when he called on him to pray, he would say, 'Briefly, friend Worsell'. One evening, after he had been going for some time, someone pulled his coat tail. He turned and said, 'Don't do that, you will quench the Spirit!' How careful we should be not to weary our hearers! This same pastor said something I have never forgotten, and try to follow in practice in my ministry. He said, 'I made up my mind when I entered the ministry, I would not get into a rut in prayer'.

George Mann was another supply who came several times a year; he was a fine man and seemed to nearly fill the doorway when he came out of the vestry. He had a nice white beard, and was always well turned out. He was preaching on one occasion and they had forgotten to put a glass of water for him. Feeling thirsty, he stopped preaching and said, 'Friends you do not muzzle the ox, but you keep him very short of water!' I once had the same experience and used the same formula, which quickly sent one of the ladies to supply the need!

Mr Mann said once when he got up to preach, 'Friends, I know my text, "The election hath obtained it, but the rest were blinded", but I do not know where to find it'. Someone soon enlightened him as to where this Scripture was to be found. He had been a miller, and there was another man by the name of King who attended in the afternoon and who was also a miller. George Mann used to get very warmed up when preaching, and one afternoon shouted, 'I'm sick of professors' (*i.e.* nominal Christians), bringing his fist down with a terrible bang on the Bible. He said at tea-time, 'I think I woke friend King up this afternoon. I expect he thought it was the bell to say that the hopper was empty!' – something that happens in old windmills.

Another minister nearly had the congregation laughing – something that was strictly forbidden – when he related a story about a minister going to visit in a 'poor house'. He asked the men there what he should pray for, and one old boy said, 'Pray that we have some more gravy, pray that we have some more gravy' – temporal needs as well as spiritual!

Another dear brother who had considerable difficulty

with pronunciation was reading the account of the Hebrew children and the image that Nebuchadnezzar set up, when he came to the list of instruments sounded. He struggled through them, and when a few verses later, he was again confronted with them, said, 'The same band, friends', and moved on!

Then there was brother Oxlade. He used to start his sermon slowly and quietly, but gradually increased, both in speed and in volume, until it was a rush of words in the same loud monotone. I used to think of the words of Holy Writ when he concluded, 'there was a great calm'. No wonder the congregation was sometimes a little restless. I remember my Uncle John who lived to be ninety-two; when he wanted to glance up at the clock hanging on the front of the gallery, he would rub the side of his face, but we all knew what he was really doing!

To support the friends at Dallington, we usually attended the special services held there on Good Friday. We used a waggonette in those days, which carried eight, the driver and one in front, and six behind sitting face to face. We would dismount and walk up steep hills, so as not to overload the horse. The small chapel was on a main road in beautiful country, but is now closed and sold. I preached there a number of times over the years. The view from the minister's vestry, which was behind the pulpit, was lovely. The seats in those days were forms with a bar at the back, very uncomfortable for children who had no support at all! The building was always full and could get very hot at times. They sang very well, unaccompanied, very slowly, all the parts making a lovely harmony. It was said that the publican from The Swan half a mile up the road would come and stand outside on Sunday afternoons to listen to this singing. One can only contrast that grand harmony with some of the 'ditties', as Dr Martyn Lloyd-Jones used to call the modern choruses! Another memory of Good Fridays is that we could pick cowslips, which grew on the light soil at Dallington, but never with us.

Another high day in the chapel calendar was August Bank Holiday. There was a tiny chapel at Magham Down, a small local village, and that was the day for their special services. Because the building was so small, the services were held in a large barn on an adjoining farm. This was cleared and straw put down on the floor; the pulpit and pews were taken up there, and set up for worship. People came in their horse-drawn vehicles from quite great distances. Sometimes there were two or three landaus – carriages with a coachman on the box. Tea was served between the services; for children, there was the added attraction of animals around the farmyard.

There was another family, something like that at Bethany – Sarah, Sally and Bill Gander, a brother and two sisters. They were not well off and lived in a small bungalow in the so-called Back Lane. The brother was a farm labourer, who was punctual to a fault; he worked for my grandfather and was never a minute late, but on the other hand, if he was at the other end of the farm doing a task which required another five minutes, he would leave for home and go all the way back the next morning to complete it! This sometimes angered my grandfather but nothing could be said.

I acted as bearer at his funeral to save expense. The service was taken by Joe Billeness from Eastbourne who had a glass business, but was a poor preacher. I thought it was rather unfair that they would not have him to preach, but would use him for funerals! But Joe was a very humble man and never seemed to take offence. He always read the same portions of Scripture, and seemed to say much the same. It was a lesson to me when taking funerals, not to fall into the same form, which seemed to me to have little effect, so I have always taken a suitable portion of the Word and sought to expound it.

Besides our summer outing, usually to a field to play games etc., we had our Sunday school winter treat, where we gathered in the afternoon, recited poems, hymns and portions of Scripture, and a minister gave us an address. After tea and the gift of an orange and some sweets, we sat for our evening service, going home in the dark in our horse-drawn Raleigh trap, with two lamps lit by candles. For years we had a very nice black mare who had been 'cast' (*i.e.* disqualified for use) in the 1914–18 war because her back was too short. She had an uneven trot, and our farm dog would recognise this on a clear night a mile from home and would start barking. Her name was Bess, and I enjoyed driving her; we kept her until in old age we had her put down. I was not excited when we replaced our horse-drawn trap for the motor car!

These people have all gone the way of all the earth, but our great mercy is that God changes not, but is the same yesterday, today and forever.

3

Stern Realities

After leaving school, I spent a year with Allwood Bros., the leading carnation specialists in those days; this involved leaving home and going into lodgings at Wivelsfield in Sussex where their main horticultural nursery was. Unknown to me, the man with whom I lodged was a drunkard, and my eyes were opened to see the terrible evil of alcohol addiction. What I witnessed in that home was very sad.

I attended the Gospel Standard chapel in Haywards Heath. My circumstances were not very pleasant, but I only remember one old lady speaking to me. No-one ever offered me any hospitality. Thirty years later, after I had entered the ministry, I was invited to speak at a young people's meeting (which no longer continues) at this same chapel. I addressed them on Hebrews 13:2, 'Be not forgetful to entertain strangers, for thereby some have entertained angels unawares', and included reference to my experience of thirty years earlier! I was not invited again.

After a year at Wivelsfield, I returned home and worked at a mixed horticultural nursery for a further twelve months. This entailed a six-mile journey each way, and I had to get to work at 7 a.m. I enjoyed my experiences and was gaining a knowledge of a wide range of plants. My brother and I saved all we could and having the princely sum of £12, we erected a small lean-to greenhouse and started growing bedding plants and cut flowers. My father was still farming Tilley Farm, about 150 acres, but our hearts were in horticulture. We had a measure of success, which really kept the farm going and, as already mentioned, our mother took in paying guests, so we came through the terrible depression of the 1930s.

During this time, I fell in love with a girl who came to stay with us; she was quite young, I was twenty-one. It was soon broken off but for about five years I prayed that our relationship might be restored. That was not to be and I believe God used the disappointment to deepen His work within my soul. I lived very near to Him, and often found real help and comfort in worship. I used to rise early on Sunday morning, do my work, and walk one-and-three-quarter miles to the chapel. During these years, I confided in a minister who frequently preached for us. In one letter he asked me if I was exercised about the ministry; my reply was, 'Although I dare not say that I am, I cannot deny that I have often had thoughts about it'. He soon accepted the pastorate of another church and I had no more correspondence with him for about fifteen years.

After that period, which I looked upon as my first love (*Rev.* 2:4), my heart gradually grew cold, and although I still attended worship on Sundays, I became very much immersed in the world. In that spiritual condition, I met and married my wife, although to my surprise, I made it clear to her that my religion came before anything else!

At the outbreak of war in 1939, we were in business flower growing and landscape gardening in a fairly big way, employing a staff of several men. The bottom fell out of our market overnight and everything had to go. In the glasshouses we were only allowed to grow tomatoes. Our financial position was difficult; the farm had been losing money and we sank deep in debt. How we proved the fact that our heavenly Father knows all our needs and can supply in unexpected ways. That first year, we grew about a quarter acre of tomatoes outdoors, always a risky crop. The weather was ideal, the demand was good, and we made enough money from that crop to pay off some of our debts and begin to readjust.

As father was ageing, we decided that we must put our energies into the farm. It was very run-down with little equipment and poor stock. We agreed to found a pedigree British Friesian herd, and purchased some excellent foundation stock from a breeder in West Sussex, including one of his home-bred bulls. This animal proved to be the most productive Friesian bull for butterfat one year in the National Milk Records (calculated on the butterfat content of all his recorded daughters).

The war brought many changes. My brother and I served in a secret unit of the Home Guard and did our share of night watching for fires. The farm was only about ten miles from the coast in what became known as 'Doodle Bug Alley'. We were subjected to hit-and-run raids by German planes which would sometimes use their guns to spray the countryside with bullets. Perhaps because we had an anti-aircraft gun positioned on the farm, a number of bombs fell around us, shattering a lot of glass from our farmhouse and glasshouses. One mine was dropped quite close, but went deep into the ground; otherwise the whole farmhouse and buildings must have been destroyed.

These events stirred us up spiritually, both personally and in the church. We began special prayer meetings, whereas before there had only been the two normal services on Sundays. My elder sister was at this time living in Croydon, and the first time she and her husband came home, she looked dreadful, having had little sleep during many nights of enemy bombing. The outcome was that they came to live at the farm until they eventually built a house and settled in the country. Although I had not made an open profession of faith in Christ, I did pray publicly on several occasions, and some who listened felt that the Lord was preparing me for His service.

As the pedigree herd increased, I became more and more involved; pedigree breeding can become very fascinating, planning the matings to produce what is hoped will be better animals. Our herd was fairly inbred, so that when other breeders used our bulls they left their stamp on a herd. Most of our animals were sold to what we called 'hobby' farmers – men who had other interests and incomes, so were in a position to pay high prices. This involved me in social activities and I became the editor of The South Eastern British Friesians Breeders' Club, but as these men were completely worldly and our meetings were mostly held in hotels, this was not good for my spiritual health. I became formal in my Christian life.

On one occasion only, I stayed away from worship on Sunday to show a judge a cow that was to be inspected for the register. I believe that the Lord marked this and it seemed to me that the judge turned against me. The Lord taught me many lessons even through the herd.

I will record one instance. We had two cows, full sisters, and we mated them to their brother. The first resulting bull made a very high price at the Reading sales where most pedigree animals in the south were sold. The following year we had a bull calf by the other sister. We had to register the birth by a card, showing the date of birth, markings etc. The date of birth for the annual show and sale went to 31 December. This calf was actually born in the early hours of 1 January, so did not quite qualify, but as it was only a matter of hours and no-one else could know, I entered it as 31 December on the card! It grew very well and was duly entered for the next annual event. As one of the youngest animals it was almost the last to be sold. It was a two-day event, the show the first and the sale the second. Our bull did not go into the sale ring until about 4 p.m. We had put a modest reserve price on it, but it was not sold. I said to my brother as I led it out of the ring, 'I know why this bull did not sell; it should never have been here'. God knew, and I had to prove the verse, 'Be sure your sins will find you out'.

Both my wife and my brother's wife came to us as landgirls in the war and in due time were converted. I was married on 8 September 1945, and my brother the following year. Many changes took place; we rented extra land, but one of the difficulties was that three families were living off the farm and this was really more than it could support.

About 1955 God began to deal with me and the backslidden state in which I had been for several years. There was first the loss of a valuable cow and her unborn calf when she broke her leg. When this happened I felt I must be silent, believing that God was speaking to me, telling me that my idol (which the herd had become) must go. I well remember one morning when my brother and I were having a cup of tea before our early milking. I said to him, 'I feel now as I have not felt for years, and can say, "He restoreth my soul'". His immediate reply was, 'Then I hope you will soon be baptised'. This created spiritual concern and I began to pray that God would show me the way. We had been taught from the pulpit that we must have a word from the Lord in all important matters. I did not remember the subject of baptism ever being preached, but now it was mentioned in a number of sermons. I felt I must speak to my father, who was the deacon, and I did so. I gave my testimony before the church and was accepted for baptism and church membership.

There was little to encourage me to take this step for there had not been a baptism for some years, and the members were all over seventy years of age. I remember the devil suggesting that it would only be a few years before I would stand alone. How true the Scripture, 'He was a liar from the beginning'. I came before the church, but was not baptised until 31 May 1956. The main reason for the delay was that my mother had been in hospital for many weeks with her second thrombosis, and it was hoped that, by waiting, she might be present. But although she was out of hospital by that date, she was unable to attend. She sent me two texts of Scripture, 'Be clothed with humility' and 'Endure hardness as a good soldier of Jesus Christ'. The first I felt I needed then, but it was some years before I proved the need of the second.

4

Call and Entrance into the Ministry

The minister who had written to me about fifteen years earlier baptised me in the presence of a chapel filled with friends and wellwishers. Soon after, he wrote to me, inquiring if I was seriously concerned about entering the ministry. I could not deny this and it duly increased my concern. In the letter, he mentioned something about my brother, whom I told about this, but said the letter contained some personal matters about myself. He said, 'If it is about the ministry, I have believed for years you would enter it'. There were others who afterwards told me that they had had the same impression, although I had never mentioned it to anyone except the one minister.

I remember staying at a Christian guest house in Bournemouth when a young man whom I had never seen before asked me if I was in the ministry. When I said 'No', he replied, 'If ever the call comes be sure you do not refuse it'. These things only increased my concern. During the summer after my baptism I prayed that if this concern was not of God, He would take it away and forgive my presumption for ever thinking of it. In the autumn of that year, it seemed as if God took that prayer away and instead I had to pray that He would prepare me for it.

Perhaps I should add here that among this group of churches, it was not felt needful to have any formal training for the ministry; the all-important matter was to have a call from God and the approval of the church. When men sat under a gracious ministry that was some preparation, but there is no doubt that some training is helpful, even if only in the mechanics of preaching. It does seem to me that today with the availability of conferences and other means of help it is not imperative for men to attend college, but if men enter the ministry without hearing the truth clearly taught much harm can ensue. In this sphere, as in all others, God is sovereign and His ways past finding out. He can use whatever instruments He pleases.

A few days before Christmas in 1956 I had a letter from a lady who largely ran the small chapel at Ninfield, a few miles from us; she was also a member at Bodle Street where I was a member. Her request was that as they had no minister for the last Sunday of the year, I should come up in the morning and assist them. There would be about eight elderly folk. Knowing the concern that I felt, it put me under great strain. I took the letter to my bedroom, fell on my knees and begged the Lord to direct me. After praying earnestly I opened my Bible at Romans 16:1–2 and read, 'I commend unto you Phebe our sister, which is a servant of the church which is at Cenchrea: that you receive her in the Lord, as becometh saints, and that ye assist her in whatsoever business she hath need of you: for she hath been a succourer of many, and of myself also'. Nothing could have more accurately described the case or have directed me more clearly. I wrote and said that, God willing, I would come. So on the last Sunday in 1956 I rode my bicycle to Ninfield Chapel.

When I arrived, the friend was sitting alone in the chapel and after greeting me asked if I had brought anything to 'read' (reading sermons was the norm for those not recognised as pastors). When I replied in the negative, she said that I could find some printed sermons in the pew. I said, 'Would you like me to read you a sermon, or as the Lord should help, to speak a few things to you?' She just broke down and wept saying, 'I have been praying for this for years'. She said that she must consult the rest of the congregation, which she did on their arrival, and it was agreed that I should address them. I did not go into the pulpit but spoke to them from the desk for some thirty to forty minutes from Colossians 1:28–29, 'Whom we preach, warning every man, and teaching every man in all wisdom; that we may present every man perfect in Christ Jesus: whereunto I also labour, striving according to his working, which worketh in me mightily'. After over thirty-five years in the ministry, that is still my one aim, to preach Christ and Him crucified as the only Saviour of men.

I returned home and told my mother and father, who was the deacon at Bodle Street. I said that I desired that things might be done in order, and that I was ready to recount my spiritual concerns and seek the church's approval, but added that even if the church could not give it, I felt that I must still preach. 'Woe is me, if I preach not the gospel' was now a reality to me. It was like a fire in my bones.

The friend at Ninfield had a great friend at Robertsbridge, another small church, and I soon received an invitation to preach there in three weeks' time. That was the first time I had entered a pulpit. I preached twice from

Acts 16:32. The opening hymn began:

> *With heavenly power, O Lord, defend*
> *Him whom we now to Thee commend*
> *His person bless, his soul secure,*
> *And make him to the end endure.*

At the end of the day, the friend who had invited me said, 'I feel I can receive you as a servant of the Lord'. For many years there was a close bond between us. Soon after this, she gave me £1 as a token of her Christian love. She was very pleased when I said that I would use it to buy a dictionary. Later she kindly wrote in it for me and I have used it all through the years.

Invitations soon came from several churches. In due time I went before my own church on Sunday 3 February 1957. Mr George Tingley preached in the morning, and I preached in the afternoon from 1 John 4:6. Mr Tingley presided over the church meeting.

Previously, I had had an invitation to take a Sunday at Ramsgate as a minister had died suddenly and left them with sixteen vacant Sundays. Although I gave them two or three dates later in the year, I did not offer them any that were more immediate. After I had written to them, the Lord applied Esther 4:14. No word has ever made me tremble as that did. The Lord showed me that I had escaped as it were by the skin of my teeth. I had not altogether held my peace. After the church meeting, Mr Tingley asked me if I would supply at Aldershot on 18 February. After the solemn word I had received from the Lord, I dared not refuse.

Aldershot and Ramsgate were the same distance from my

house, one east and the other west, both entailing my being driven to Eastbourne or Hastings to take a train as we lived half-way between these two towns. Before I entered the ministry, I made the only vow I have ever made in my life, that I would preach wherever the Lord opened doors. At times that has brought me into difficulties, especially with the Gospel Standard, but I could not let anything break that solemn vow.

Soon, invitations came from many parts of the country. I never had a free Sunday for years and was often preaching during the week as well. Within a year or so, I had my first spiritual child, although I did not know it until about three years later. What a great joy it is to a minister when God gives him converts! I was preaching in one of the smallest Strict Baptist chapels where only evening services were held. As was often the case, the chapel was full. A girl of about thirteen years of age came that evening for two reasons only – she had never attended the tiny chapel and she had not heard this new preacher. My subject was, 'The wise and the foolish virgins'. She said that she went out feeling she was only a foolish virgin. She later joined a large Gospel Standard church and married a minister.

On one of my train journeys to Ramsgate, I had to change at Ashford where I met Mr W. Gibb, who was the senior deacon as well as a minister of Jireh Chapel, Tenterden. He asked me if I had any vacant dates. I said that I had one, the first Sunday in September 1957. On consulting his diary he said that Mr Hayler (pastor at Folkestone) was engaged, but his health was very uncertain, so I was asked if I would book the date, subject to his being unable to fulfil it. This I did, but soon after had another invitation to preach on the same date at Haydock in the north, which I accepted if I was not needed at Tenterden. The outcome was that I came to Tenterden on Sunday 1 September 1957 and preached twice from the text, 'It is not in me' (*Gen.* 41:16). I was a complete stranger to them.

5
Itinerant Ministry

The largest congregation that I have preached to was upwards of five hundred in a large Congregational church in Cleveleys, near Blackpool, Lancashire, at a Northern Choirs gathering. My text on that occasion was, 'Bring me a minstrel' (*2 Kings* 3:15). The smallest was a Fen village to two people who lived in the chapel house, rent free, on the condition that they cared for the chapel and had one service weekly. That was a very disheartening congregation for they had no interest in the gospel.

One of my first long-distance engagements has always remained a vivid memory. It was at Swanwick Shore, near Southampton, a distance of 107 miles from my home. The engagement was in February, and the weather was cold and snowy. I had a Ford Prefect with no heater, so I needed a rug to wrap round my legs. I arrived at Vine Cottage, my destination, after a heavy fall of snow. The cottage was down a lane and about one hundred yards through a long garden, where I found the inhabitants, Mr and Mrs Bevis. He said I must leave my car in his cousin's garden in the open. We returned and sat around a kitchen range in the living room. Supper was fat bacon and bread, but by the end of the evening, I felt we had known each other for years, as we talked of the things of God. Bedtime came early, and I followed my host upstairs by candlelight, not knowing what awaited me! The walls were brick on edge, *i.e.* four-and-a-half inches thick. The father of Mrs Bevis, a Mr Harding, had been the first and only pastor of the church. He worked for a brickmaker, and when money was short, sometimes had to take bricks instead of money, so the cottage had been built of these.

When in bed, I found the bedclothes very thin and wondered if circumstances were the same as when the cottage was built! It was a bitterly cold night, and I could not sleep because I was so cold. I worried that my car would be frozen in the morning, so what with those things and the concern about the preaching the next day, it seemed one of the longest and coldest nights I can ever remember. I survived, glad to be strengthened with more fat bacon in the morning. I believe my preaching warmed hearts that day, for I soon received an invitation to preach at their special services on the Easter Monday. These were the first I ever took, and I continued to preach at them for some years. The Bevises were a godly couple. He had lost his eardrums in the First World War, 1914–1918, so could not hear a sound! I continued to preach there for many years.

My first preaching engagement in London was at Kilburn, where I stayed with an old couple in the house at the back of the chapel. They had been members of the church for over sixty years, and had three single daughters living with them. The house consisted of two or three storeys and the toilet was on the ground floor, which meant descending and ascending two or three flights of stairs if the body called for relief in the night! I always felt touched, when I as a young man sat in the vestry before the service, and this venerable old gentleman came and knelt by me to plead for God's blessing on our worship. There was a thermometer hanging by the pulpit which he often consulted. I remember another old chap saying to me, 'If you complain about the heating, you get the thermometer thrown at you'. There were forty to fifty attending when I first went, but they died off and the chapel has been closed for many years now.

A very different setting was a chapel at Pell Green, near Wadhurst. The chapel was built right on the roadside, the pulpit on the wall facing away from the road. Two brothers by the name of Thunder had been there for many years. One was unmarried and lived in a cottage adjoining, and I understood that everything there was kept just as it was when his mother died. He was rather eccentric. He always sat in the gallery, and you could hardly say 'Amen' before he was down the stairs and out of the door. I made a rule that I would not preach on the first Sunday in the month, if they did not have the communion. Unknowingly I had booked such a Sunday with them, so did not renew that date. The next year when he paid me – he used almost to thrust the 10s. (50p) at you – he said, 'You docked us one this year!' I suppose that was better than saying they did not want me again! This chapel also is now closed.

Two miles away was another chapel, Shovers Green, where I preached. The design was similar, but the pulpit was on the opposite wall, so that the preacher could see the traffic going past. I understand that, years ago, a man was preaching when he suddenly burst out laughing. It seems that a man was just riding past on a donkey when the animal tossed him over its head, and the sight was just too much for the preacher! Sadly, this chapel is now a private residence, albeit very attractive.

At Lamberhurst was another small chapel where I spent some Sundays. Here were two other brothers, woodcutters, who lived in a cottage in the woods; their names were Manasseh and Ephraim. They never married and were quite quaint. Here we always had our meal around the slow-combustion stove; then I would return to the minister's vestry. I remember going there to a Good Friday service before I entered the ministry. The hymn before the sermon began was chosen and announced by the deacon – 'Hark how the Gospel trumpet sounds' . The minister said to me afterwards, 'I thought our friend was a little premature this evening!'.

I sometimes ministered in a chapel which had a very low pulpit and where the people sat on forms. Water was brought in a bottle. On one occasion when I wanted a drink while speaking, I noticed there was a dead spider in the glass, so felt it wiser to leave my thirst unquenched, not knowing how long the water had been there, or how poisonous the spider might be!

For a few years I had six to eight engagements at Ramsgate Strict Baptist chapel, long since closed and sold; I could almost write a book on my experiences there! I remember one Sunday morning after preaching, I felt so ashamed of my ministry that I went straight into the vestry and waited, hoping that all the congregation had dispersed; but to my amazement, when I did venture out, there were three people waiting to tell me how God had blessed them through the sermon! Although painful, that is perhaps better than when the preacher thinks he has done well, although the people are unmoved.

At Ramsgate, I used to lodge with a Miss Nugent, who was one of four sisters (I knew them all well); their father had been a pastor in a Strict Baptist church in Balham, London. This sister kept a boarding house at Pegwell Bay on the outskirts of Ramsgate. It overlooked the sea, and the rooms were large and lofty. It was a drive of seventy miles from my home, pleasant in the summer, but could be rather an ordeal in the winter. My hostess wore a number of layers of woollies, so did not feel the cold. Sometimes my visits would be in very cold weather and she had hardly any fire. One evening when she went to make a drink, I put on some sticks which were on the tiles. When she saw the blaze, she said, 'You haven't used that wood, have you? That's for lighting in the morning'. I had humbly to answer, 'Yes, Miss Nugent'.

She used to have a bed-warming pan, and would take the fire's remaining embers, put them in the pan to warm your bed, then come down and talk for another twenty minutes, so you would end up having neither a fire nor a warm bed! On one occasion she said, 'This is your seventh visit; next time you will have a clean towel'. I envisaged towels labelled with various ministers' names and being ticked off at each visit!

She was a very gracious soul and I enjoyed my visits. In the summer there would be thirty to forty visitors staying in the two houses that she ran. Nothing ever seemed to bother her; for instance, if there were not enough boiled eggs to go round, she would just say at breakfast, 'To-morrow we will start and go round the other way'. One friend, when asked if he enjoyed his holiday there, said he thought it was an endurance test!

One pastor for whom I had a great regard would listen to

any young man in his congregation who felt he had a call to the ministry. He would then visit the man's wife, point out any undesirable practices and say, 'You are his wife, so you are the one to tell him, so that it does not become a habit' – very valuable advice. My late dear friend, George Rose (1874–1965), used to come and hear me and would often point out things which I should note and discard, so he was a very real help. He used to say, 'Bernard, nothing but the best is good enough for the Lord'. How true. We cannot make the Word effective, but there are the mechanics of preaching, by which we can present the gospel in the best possible manner.

For many years, I made an annual preaching tour of the north, where I met some unusual characters. At Southport, there was a Mrs Hampson with whom I always stayed. She had a husband, Albert; a policeman from the Shetland Islands also lived with them. She took him in as a lodger for two weeks, on condition that he went with her to worship. Jock stayed for the rest of his life! He had little to say, but she was very anxious that he should pray at the prayer meeting. She said, 'All you have to do is stand up, and God will give you the words'. After much persuading, one evening he stood up, but no words came! After that, he always remained silent. Albert and Jock used to go off to bed leaving us installed in two rocking chairs by the fire. It was then that her stories and the experiences began, and one had to be content to stay until the early hours of the morning before retiring. She was a great one for herbs, doctoring you for whatever you were in need of! One brother said to me, 'I do not know which is worse, the malady, or the remedy!'

When I first preached at Blackpool, I stayed with an

elderly lady, and I never drank so many cups of tea any-where. It was tea when you arrived, before you had a nap, after you woke up, before you went out, when you came in, when you retired for the night and before you arose in the morning, beside all meal times!

I remember an old lady at Swavesey in Cambridgeshire. If we had enjoyed a good day at worship, she would say when we were back at her home, laying her hand on her heart, 'I feel so warm here'. For some years, this trip ended with two sermons on Good Friday at Sharnbrook in Bedfordshire. There were only a handful that attended the Sunday afternoon services, but on these occasions folk would come from chapels around, and the place would be nearly full. It was a large chapel, and I believe many were helped and blessed over the years; I often felt much liberty in preaching. I would return and stay with a Mr and Miss Northern, who farmed in a big way. Many friends would be invited for an evening meal and a time of sweet fellowship together.

After leaving Jireh, Tenterden, I had engagements at Hanover, Tunbridge Wells, the Gospel Standard cause in the town. On one such evening engagement I took with me one of my deacons and his wife. On our return journey, he said, 'I do not think you will get your cards[1] here after this evening'. I said, 'We will have to wait and see!' I continued to preach there for about another three years. I knew the church was divided, some saying I should not be asked, because I was not in agreement with some of their Articles of Faith, others wanting still to enjoy my ministry. There were two deacons, one favourable, and one not. When the

[1] i.e., be banned from preaching.

'unfavourable' deacon left the room before the service, the 'favourable' said, 'I suppose you know this is your last visit!' – very helpful news, as one was about to preach to them!

I said I presumed it would be so. I preached from Paul's farewell speech to the Ephesian elders (*Acts* 20:32). How true are God's words, 'I am he that shutteth and no man openeth, and openeth and no man shutteth'. How good if we can accept this in all our experiences.

In those days, Strict Baptist ministers were often very poorly paid. There might have been an excuse for struggling causes, but alas, it seemed to apply in the larger churches. I once preached at the anniversary services in a large Midlands church, three services on a Sunday, and the chapel was full with upwards of three hundred. Before the evening service, a deacon said to me in the vestry, 'Our collections are not quite up to the usual. You will know how to put it, but just remind them of the fact', which I did. When I got home, I found my *expenses* had hardly been met! That church is almost ready to close. I also knew that they had treated one of their pastors in what I considered was a disgraceful manner.

One of my most memorable weekends was when I preached for my late dear brother, Tom Tuitt, a West Indian, in the East End of London.

When we arrived at the hall where worship was to be held, Tom was alone, doing some tidying up. We discussed the services and agreed that he would conduct and I would pray and preach. He said I was at liberty to preach for as long as I liked, but his people expected him to preach for at least an hour. There was a door at the back of the hall and one about half-way down the side. About three minutes before the time of the service they poured in through both doors and filled the building, some 140–150 folk, all West Indian. They began with two or three hymns and took an offering, etc. It was all rather new to me, but I realised it was their culture. I have always felt it was unwise to force a mode of worship on a different culture, *e.g.* imposing the mode in the Highlands of Scotland upon those of another race. I believe both modes are pleasing to God if they are sincere. I preached in the morning from, 'O Lord, by these things men live, and in all things is the life of my spirit' (*Isa.* 38:16). There were various responses, and at the end of the sermon a lady sitting close shouted such a loud 'Amen' it made me jump! Very different from the absolute silence that I had been brought up in! Tom said to me afterwards, 'It is a long time since I cried so much in church, and I have never seen my organist in tears before'. The service was partly a testimony and I believe it touched many hearts as I related many of my own experiences.

In the afternoon, Tom drove me to a hospital to visit one of my deacons; it was a sweet time of fellowship in the gospel. My deacon *never* forgot it. Tom and his wife visited him during the following week and quite embarrassed him with their love and gifts. I said to Tom, 'I suppose you do a lot of hospital visiting?' 'No', he replied, 'our people are very healthy'. Although they arrived just in time for worship, they were in no hurry to go afterwards, and instead of a handshake from some it was a huge embrace!

A few years after my visit Tom came and preached at our anniversary services at Trinity, and I believe enjoyed his visit as much as I had done mine. We then used *Gospel Hymns*, and I remember how thrilled he was with the great old hymns with their fine doctrinal content. When he announced them he said, with much expression and delight,

'Now let us sing another of these lovely gospel hymns'. Dear Tom was truly Reformed, and for many years preached faithfully in East London, beginning, I believe, in a railway hut. He knew much opposition in his early days, but God stood by him. What a joy it will be to meet him again in glory.

The church at Bounds Cross, Biddenden, Kent has had an interesting history, and I have several experiences and memories connected with it. I baptised two or three people there, one a girl in her late teens; to economise, their heating was on 'off peak'. It was the dead of winter, and on the evening I baptised her it did not come on until the service was under way. She told me afterwards that her teeth chattered during the sermon; I then had to baptise her in very cold water, and then there was no heat in the room in which she had to change! It certainly was a rather trying ordeal, and sprinkling would have been more comfortable if I could have believed it was really the example our dear Lord had set.

The first pastor at Bounds Cross, John Kemp, I knew very well as he often came and preached for us at Bodle Street. He was asked to accept the pastorate without any congregation, while the chapel was being built. When he commenced to preach, the people gathered, and for years he preached to a well-filled chapel. He ministered there for over fifty years. I remember attending his jubilee services when about 1,000 people were present. They erected a marquee for the overflow and had three services. Pastor Walter Brooke of West Street Chapel, Croydon preached in the morning, John Kemp in the afternoon, and Pastor J. K. Popham of Galeed, Brighton in the evening. They had a policeman to conduct the traffic, and I remember one minister commenting, 'I expect people are surprised and are saying, "We thought all these Calvinists were dead!"'

John Kemp was one of five pastors I knew personally who held pastorates for more than fifty years. In the case of Stanley Delves of Crowborough, his predecessor was also in the office for over fifty years, so the two spanned over a century. It has been my observation that when men have continued so long, they can unwittingly become dictators. A generation grows up under their ministry and pastoral care, and their word can become law. I knew of one case where a church meeting was mentioned and the pastor said, '*I* will say when we are to have a church meeting'. Sometimes such leaders make no provision for the future when they are taken, in some cases with very sad results.

One piece of advice given to me by an old lady soon after I commenced my ministry was, 'Always be yourself in the pulpit'. That was sound advice much needed in some quarters! God does not expect us to put on some special tone of voice and manner and act unnaturally.

I seldom preached in Essex, but used to visit one chapel. I stayed with some friends who had the most uncomfortable bed I ever slept on; however you lay, it seemed that a lump was pressing into you. I think they called them flock mattresses, but in this one, all the flocks seemed to be fighting one another, which did not tend to a very restful night!

In this chapter, I have given some different experiences encountered in preaching the gospel. Some were not easy or pleasant, and added to the burdens and cares of the most terrible and glorious calling a man can exercise – 'standing between the living and the dead'. One is dealing with matters concerning immortal souls, for an eternity in heaven in matchless bliss and joy unspeakable, or hell in indescribable torments, which after a million years will not be one second nearer the end. May all my readers pray much and earnestly for all whom God calls to preach the unsearchable riches of Christ, that they may be faithful, always having a single eye to the glory of God.

For many years, I have always set aside a time on Sunday morning to pray for all my brethren in the ministry, both in this country and abroad; only eternity will reveal what has been done through prayer.

I believe Joseph Hart sums it up well:

> *Prayer was appointed to convey*
> *The blessings God designed to give,*
> *Long as they live should Christians pray;*
> *For only while they pray they live.*

6

Pastorate at Jireh, Tenterden

I have already referred to the Sunday in 1957 when I first preached at Jireh Chapel, Tenterden, Kent. There were some that day who felt persuaded I should become their pastor. They had been pastorless for thirty-eight years. I believe it is true to say that there was a division among them, although I was blissfully unaware of it. Partly as a result of my first visit, there was an application by a young person for baptism and church membership. On being asked whom she would like to baptise her, she requested that I might do so. I accepted the invitation and took the baptismal service on 15 January 1959. The chapel was comfortably filled, with four ministers present. I preached from Romans 6:3–4 and gave our dear friend Psalm 37:5, 'Commit thy way unto the Lord; trust also in Him; and He shall bring it to pass'. She has remained a loyal friend all these years and our younger son married her only daughter, which has been a great joy to us. They have two lovely children. Our friend has had a painful path to walk for many years, but the grace of God has shone brightly in her.

Partly as a result of my second visit to Tenterden, I received an invitation to supply their pulpit for the first three months of 1960 'with a view' to the pastorate. At that time I was preaching fairly frequently at Tamworth Road Chapel, Croydon and believe the Lord used my ministry for the conversion of some and the building up of others. It was always a pleasure to preach there as my dear friend, George Rose, had been a former pastor and was greatly used of God. The chapel, which held about three hundred, was usually full in his time.

I used to go to the prayer meeting at Tamworth Road on a Saturday evening. The senior deacon was a very gracious and humble man, Mr A. Russell, and we often spent sweet times of fellowship together. I did not know if I might have a call from them, but in looking back I can see that I was better suited to a country church than a town situation.

After my invitation to Tenterden, I preached for them on a number of evenings during the week. I accepted their proposal and preached for the first three months of 1960 both on Sundays and in the week. During this time I visited the members of the church and congregation, so getting to know them personally. I felt liberty in preaching and a growing love for them during these months. I was to give a reply as to my decision on their call by the end of June. In many ways acceptance was not easy as I had commitments to my father and brother. It would entail the disposal of our farm and herd, something I said I would never do. As time went by and they expected the answer, the words seemed impressed upon my mind, 'Be still and know that I am God'. I am sure many earnest prayers were ascending both from the congregation and from myself.

One evening at this time, I took one of the deacons and his sister home and as they alighted, he said, 'If you do not become our pastor, I do not know what we shall do'. After further prayerful consideration I felt that I must accept. So I wrote to the church agreeing, but on one condition, that I commence the pastorate with a week of prayer, and they were willing to accept this condition.

The farm and arrangements for the families had next to be settled. Father was unable to carry on and my brother felt he wanted to leave the farm, so it was agreed to sell the property, the livestock and the equipment. My elder sister agreed to take and care for our mother and father. My brother purchased the Old Mill House and sixteen acres of land at Boreham Street, about a mile from the farm as the crow flies. I was now free to go to Tenterden.

Our farm did not realise what we had hoped and when all the debts and expenses were met, we were left with only a few thousand pounds each. My next difficulty was finding a house in Tenterden; a number were inspected but nothing seemed suitable. The chapel owned two adjoining houses, but both had tenants who were members of the church and I was not prepared to turn them out. After some time two members of the congregation offered to give £1,000 towards a house. Later they said they would purchase one, and we could live in it rent free. Soon after this a suitable property came on the market and they purchased it for £4,500. So God graciously provided and we were settled in about mid-January.

As agreed, we held a prayer meeting each evening of the first week of my pastorate; this included the New Year services on 4 January 1961, when the congregation was larger than for some years. A different pastor from the neighbouring churches gave an address each evening. The numbers attending varied from about 90 to 130.

At the close of the week Mr W. Gibb said to me, 'I

believe I can accept you as my pastor, and if the Lord will come and bless my soul, I can say, "Lord, now lettest Thou thy servant depart in peace"'. I felt humbled. My dear friend, George Rose, had said to me, 'Mr Gibb is an elder; stand beside him, but do not step before him'. I believed that to be good advice and tried to carry it out. Mr Gibb lived for another two or three years and I do not remember any difference between us, although he may not always have agreed with me.

The text for my first Sunday was Psalm 118:24–25 at both services: 'This is the day which the Lord hath made; we will rejoice and be glad in it. Save now, I beseech Thee, O Lord; O Lord, I beseech Thee, send now prosperity'. The church was happy for me to preach elsewhere during the week, and as long as I visited the congregation, that was all that was required. No outreach was ever thought of. The members were also willing to adjust their week-night services to fit in with my other engagements. I preached 272 sermons that first year, and Mr George Jempson was approved for the ministry. The first two or three years were happy ones. Although there had long been a division among the people, that was covered up, and I believe that they felt having a pastor would solve their problems. The congregation increased and two or three were added to the church, including my wife; at times with visitors there would be nearly one hundred people present.

The first ripple of discontent came when I preached on the commissions in the Gospels. On the first Sunday, I took Matthew in the morning, beginning where I believe we should, 'All power is given unto me'. In the afternoon I took Mark, 'Go ye into all the world and preach the gospel to every creature'. In the week I preached from Luke. When

I asked two members how they were after the evening service they replied, 'We feel better after this evening'. You could have knocked me down with a feather! On the Sunday, I had sought to expound the text, but as Hyper-Calvinists[1] they had no place for the gospel being preached to all! The following Sunday, I continued with the commission to Peter in John's Gospel, chapter 21, which was generally acceptable; feeding the lambs and the sheep did not give offence. These things drove me to search the Scriptures more carefully. I had no wish to give offence, but at the same time could not be bound. I suppose these years found me as loyal and united to the Gospel Standard as at any period in my life. At this time (June 1962) and at their request I allowed my name to go on the Gospel Standard list, but not before having it in writing that it did not restrict me as to where I preached, having made a vow to God before entering the ministry that I would go wherever He opened the doors.

The congregation was well balanced in age; there were elderly, some in business and with families, and quite a large Sunday school which I addressed monthly. The services on Sunday included Sunday school and morning prayer meeting followed by a service of one-and-a-half hours, a midday prayer meeting and then the afternoon service of one-and-a-half hours. Many brought their lunch, which was eaten in the chapel, with cups of tea provided. After the afternoon service I had a short rest, as for years I often took a third service in another church, sometimes travelling as far as fifty miles each way; this made a very full day.

[1] I will explain this term and the controversy surrounding it in chapter eight.

There were some godly folk in Tenterden, and my pastoral visits were often times of sweet fellowship. In looking back, it is not easy to see where the change began to take place, both in me and in the congregation. I had not been brought up in a rigid Gospel Standard situation and as I began to move more widely, I came to feel unhappy about certain things and practices in the light of Scripture. I also felt that my ministry should be more balanced, realising that if you only preach 'experience', you will soon fall into a rut.

I believe that the change in my ministry began to show when, on a Whit Sunday, I preached on Pentecost. Conscious afterwards that I had not done justice to the subject, I continued with the subject the next Sunday although I had not intended to do so. I felt so gripped with the Acts narrative that I began to preach more consecutively and systematically, seeking to expound the text more fully than had been common in our pulpits. The consecutive method was disliked by some who felt that my texts were no longer 'given' to me. I believe with hindsight that I would have been wiser to have just used consecutive exposition in one service and continued as before in the other. The fact was, the book of Acts was so exciting to me that I just wanted to bring it before the congregation.

There was also another aspect. My new practice meant that I had to face and expound matters which previously I had tended to neglect. One morning when I was dealing with the first part of Acts 6:1–6, I had the secretary of the Gospel Standard committee and his family unexpectedly in the congregation. The way in which the apostles dealt democratically with the situation was quite opposite to the way the Gospel Standard committee operated! They did not return in the afternoon and never came to hear me again.

Sadly, the division in the congregation began to show itself, yet there were many who were happy and benefiting under the ministry. Two more brethren were sent out into the ministry. In the case of one, there was some opposition and difficulty, mainly because of the two camps. But the congregation continued to increase and I often felt liberty in preaching. I had become more concerned about my sermons, believing they needed more order and structure to them. Sermon notes were strongly condemned in our tradition; it was thought that anyone who used them was clearly not relying on the Holy Spirit. My desire to have order meant memorising headings, but with upwards of three hundred sermons and addresses each year, this memorisation imposed a strain which I felt the Lord did not require when I could have a few headings on a slip of paper. I changed my practice on this point with some concern; would it bring the frown of God upon me? I felt the Lord did not disapprove and continued to use them, although in such a way that no-one would have observed it. You could be barred from a pulpit for such a fault. About this time, I sent a copy of one of my sermon notes to my friend E. J. Knight in the United States who was in a situation very similar to my own. He wrote back to say they had really gripped him.

As time went on, dissatisfaction increased in the strongest 'hypers', but those that had more recently come to attend, seemed to enjoy and profit from the ministry. Towards the end of my pastorate I began to attend the Westminster Fellowship under Dr Martyn Lloyd-Jones, and to preach more widely. On one occasion one of the deacons said he could not pray for his pastor because he was preaching with another Strict Baptist minister of whom he did not approve.

Towards what proved to be the end of my pastorate there were three applications for baptism and church membership. I felt I could receive these, but when visited by the deacons, two were turned down and they would not agree to them coming before the church. They afterwards relented in the case of one, so two gave their testimonies and were received into the church. The fact that the other one was not allowed to come caused some distress as she was the daughter of two long-standing members. At the baptism of one of these sisters, who was in her seventies, I expressed my great pleasure, but remarked that it was not really an example to follow, as we should be baptised as soon as we come to saving faith in Jesus Christ. The position in these churches is that people must reach a certain standard of experience, much beyond what the Scriptures require, in order to attain the assurance necessary (so it was believed) to make profession of faith. The service in which I was to receive these dear sisters into the church membership should have been a time of rejoicing. The deacon who chose and gave out the hymns that day began with hymn 835 (*Gadsby's*), of which the first verse reads:

> *Deep in a cold and joyless cell,*
> *A doleful gulf of gloomy care,*
> *Where dismal doubts and darkness dwell,*
> *The dangerous brink of black despair;*
> *Chilled by the icy damps of death,*
> *I feel no firm support of faith.*

A family group c.1900 – Joseph Honeysett (father) seated in the wagon, David Honeysett (grandfather) standing with shovel and John Honeysett (uncle) holding the front horse.

Left
Tilly Farm, Boreham Street, near Herstmonc
– the Honeysett family home for many years.

Right
The author (left) with his brother
Douglas and his elder sister Edith.

Bernard (left) with his brother and their stock bull, Tunley Hilkees, c.1995.

View from Tilley Farm

Gwendoline Honeysett

The opening day at Trinity Chapel, Tenterden, Kent, August 1969.

There are four verses and by the last one a glimmer of hope appeared!

Let hope survive, though damped by doubt;
Do thou defend my battered shield;
O let me never quite give out;
Help me to keep the bloody field;
Lord, look upon the unequal strife,
Delay not, lest I lose my life.

A sad situation developed in the diaconate; one deacon was very opposed to me, and one, who was not very strong, was influenced by him; the other one was in agreement with me and remained loyal until the end of his life. This made church matters in the diaconate very difficult, and a similar situation developed in the church.

About this time, a visiting minister preached one Sunday (it was my policy never to speak to another concerning church matters), and on the Monday he came to tea with me. I had been away that Sunday and when I asked him how he had got on preaching, he replied, 'I seemed to be preaching to two different congregations'.

The break came when the opposing deacon rose at a church meeting and, under 'Any Other Business', accused me of preaching against the Articles of the church; this at once caused uproar and I could only bring the meeting to a close. I prepared a statement of belief, called a deacons' meeting, and requested that a copy go to all members. In this proposed statement I wrote that if anyone could prove from Scripture that I was wrong, I was only too willing to be shown and confess my error. No deacon pointed out any error, but they said this would split the church down the middle, so I rewrote it in milder language, though without changing the meaning. It was agreed to call a special church meeting to deal with this serious situation. The Articles of the chapel were not in the trust deed, but they had been adopted, I believe, about 1926. I asked that the decision which had adopted these Articles should be rescinded. At the church meeting, the opposing deacons received a bare majority not to do so. One member attended that church meeting who had never been to a church meeting while I had been pastor; I had no doubt why she was there! This left me no alternative but to resign my pastorate, which I did with regret and sorrow on 23 April 1967. The deacons said afterwards that they felt I had taken the only honourable course. So my pastorate ended after six-and-a-half years. I told one of the deacons when he called the next morning that I believed the Lord would provide for me to continue my ministry in Tenterden, and that he would give me the use of the building owned by the Free Church of England to preach in.

It had become increasingly obvious that the Gospel Standard authorities were eagerly awaiting their opportunity to strike me off their list of ministers. They must have already had a letter drafted to that effect, for I resigned from Jireh on the Monday and the letter duly arrived by first post on the Wednesday! The only reason given for this action was that I had preached at the annual meetings of the Strict and Particular Baptist Trust Corporation – but, as I have already indicated, I had long since obtained written consent to my preaching wherever God opened doors. This unhappy breach left me open to all kinds of baseless suspicions.

I was now fifty-four years of age and another chapter in my life had closed. I had no hard feelings regarding any at

Jireh; I was only sorry that they were not willing to judge everything in the light of Scripture and to be governed entirely by it and not to be so bound by tradition. I have continued to pray for them during the years.

them, I was only sorry that they were not willing to prove
everything in the light of Scripture and to be governed
entirely by it and not to be so bound by tradition. I have
continued to pray for them during the years.

7

New Influences – Charles Haddon Spurgeon and Martyn Lloyd-Jones

As will already be clear, while I was serving Jireh
Chapel, Tenterden, between the years 1960 and
1967, some of my convictions went through a
considerable change. It was a change which involved me in
painful difficulties but I thank God for it because I know it
was His doing. There were vital parts of the Word of God
which He brought me to understand in a new way. But
God uses means, and I want to write now of two of the
preachers whose influence entered my life at this time and
who were used to contribute much to the re-thinking
which I was compelled to do. Surprisingly, perhaps, one
of these men had died twenty years before I was born. The
other had been the minister of Westminster Chapel,
London, for a quarter-of-a-century before I came to know
him. Let me speak first of Dr Lloyd-Jones.

It was about 1964 that I first attended the Ministers'
Fellowship at Westminster Chapel, started by Dr Lloyd-
Jones in 1941. His was not a name much heard in our
circles and it was even rumoured that he was 'Arminian'.
My first impression of these monthly meetings was of their

liveliness and Christian spirit. Much that I began to hear in addresses and discussions was very new to me. At times I was puzzled and left with serious questions on my mind. When you have been over forty years in a tradition it is not easy to break out. There was often something which made me query, 'Is this right?' but in those days I was very much the new boy and seldom ventured to speak.

The form of the meetings varied little. At 11 a.m. 'the Doctor' (as we all knew him) would take his chairman's seat in the upstairs lecture hall, before a table and reading desk and with his back to the radiator – always checking to be sure that the heat was turned right up! Someone would be called on to lead in prayer. One of my first memories of the Fellowship was of such an opening prayer which arrested and moved me. I had no idea who the speaker was but later learned that it was Paul Bassett whom I later came to know and esteem. After this prayer, Lloyd-Jones would proceed to ask what particular subject or question we wished to discuss. Once this was settled debate would proceed, perhaps slowly at first, and with the chairman drawing in as many contributions as possible. Next to preaching, he loved discussion. He had great skill in guiding proceedings, keeping a subject going when no one else could see a way forward, and bringing out new points when the rest of us supposed we had nearly reached a conclusion. He would not rise to his feet until he finally summed up the discussion, when he stated the main conclusions in a way which fixed them in your mind. The gesture I remember him using most was one he always employed to emphasise the importance of distinguishing 'the big thing' – raising his hands above his head and then bringing them down on either side of his body in a wide arch – from the secondary:

'We must not forget the big thing.'

He always closed in prayer himself and that prayer often seemed to bring everything into a right perspective and lift us up into the presence of God.

The composition of the Fellowship was somewhat mixed. Many of the men seemed to have moved from a theological position which was the very opposite of my own ultra-Calvinism. But for discussions to be lively and profitable, you need men with differing viewpoints. I did not always agree with Peter Lewis, yet I felt he made valuable contributions. Selwyn Morgan was another brother who was always helpful. I often observed that the Doctor and Iain Murray crossed swords; I knew that they were friends and concluded it was their different views on church government that caused the clashes! Paul Cook was another brother who often contributed; I remember the Doctor saying on one occasion after Paul Cook had been speaking, 'We want the right Paul', alluding to the apostle! An element of humour might well arise at some point in the proceedings, generally unexpectedly. Once when the subject of dreams was perhaps being treated with more respect than Dr Lloyd-Jones approved, he told us of a case in his former charge in South Wales. A woman who owned a fish-and-chip shop was concerned that he should interpret a dream she had experienced. In this dream she had seen herself going down to the shore where she was suddenly confronted by galloping horses, some on their hind legs. 'What did it mean?' she was anxious to know. 'I think,' her pastor told her, 'that you ate too many fish and chips before you went to bed!'

We often enjoyed anecdotes of this kind. On one occasion, when the discussion was on the need for patience,

Lloyd-Jones gave this illustration. A very nervous man was courting a lady who kept a shop. The courtship had gone on for some time and with no success as far as the man was concerned. Patience exhausted, he one day suddenly confronted the object of his affections when she was behind the counter of her shop and addressed her with the words, 'It is now or never'. 'With disastrous results,' the Doctor added dryly. And he went on to give us a brief personal allusion, 'I had to allow my wife time to consider whether she felt she could live with me.' Incidents from his own pastoral ministry were often particularly helpful. I recall how emphatic he was against our expecting a standardised Christian experience as though there was a stereotyped Christian. Referring to one of the fellowship meetings when he served the church at Aberavon, he told us of a night when one of the brethren present, who had been a drunkard, gave his testimony to the effect that since he had been converted, alcohol had never been a problem. As the man spoke, Lloyd-Jones noticed another man in a corner who looked downcast at what he was hearing, so he asked him, ' Mr — — what has been your experience?' The man replied, 'After what I have just heard, I wonder if I am a Christian at all, for I can never pass a public house, and smell drink, but that it is a temptation to me.' The conclusion drawn was that we cannot make hard-and-fast rules.

Often it was a comparative aside, spoken by Lloyd-Jones, which gave us new insights. For example, when discussion centred on the difference between demon possession and mental disorder and the difficulty in distinguishing between the two, he said that a demon-possessed person would always react violently to the name of Jesus Christ, but that was not so where the case was one of mental disorder.

In listening to difficulties and problems expressed by members of the Fellowship, Lloyd-Jones was very sympathetic but there were rare occasions when, if he believed a speaker was advertising himself and his own abilities, he could be severe. He rounded with a touch of anger, as well as sarcasm, on a speaker on one occasion who had told us confidently that he had no need of commentaries and that one piece of paper and a pencil was all he required on a Saturday night for his sermon preparation: 'You do not need a pencil or paper on Saturday evening, but beware of what you *think* you have been given!'

Only once do I remember our chairman having difficulty with his English. He was relating an experience in his early ministry when he was inclined to put more matter into his sermons than his hearers could well grasp. An older minister, observing this in a service at which they both spoke, commented to him afterwards in Welsh, 'Your hay was good tonight but your *rack* was too high'. In telling us this, the Doctor paused before the word 'rack', saying, 'I know the Welsh word but cannot think of the English'. Grasping the farming picture of a wooden or iron structure on a stable wall above the horses, set at a height at which they could easily eat the hay, I supplied the word he wanted and said 'rack'. 'That's it,' he went on, 'Your hay was good, but your rack was too high.'

I must not mislead the reader into thinking that Dr Lloyd-Jones commonly spoke about himself. On the contrary, his dislike of anything that drew attention to himself was often evident. Only once do I recall him speaking at any length about his own spiritual experience and that was after he returned to us after some months of illness in 1968. While he testified to having known 'the peace of God which *passeth all understanding*,' he had much to say which was both humbling to himself as well as to us. It had troubled him that he had not felt more eager for heaven and that he could not honestly say with Paul that he longed 'to depart and to be with Christ; which is far better'. When he was seventy, the Fellowship made a presentation to him through one of the older members, Edgar Wood. He almost brushed it aside, and at once got on with the business in hand. I think that at least part of his reaction on that occasion was due to the fact that our action and words affected him deeply and he did not want to show it in some emotional way. Perhaps at such times he could not quite trust himself. About two or three years after my joining the Fellowship there was a division in the evangelical scene in England and it led to a reconstituting of the Fellowship in 1966 with the exclusion of any who were in sympathy with the ecumenical movement. At that time there were a number who wanted the Doctor to take a more public position in the organisation of a new movement or denomination. But he always declined, believing that he had been called to be an evangelist. He had no interest in 'movements' as such. It was the movement of God in the current scene which he looked for and that brings me to another point about these meetings of the Fellowship which affected me at this time.

The only occasion on which the form of the meeting varied was when a speaker, probably someone from a distance, was introduced and asked to give an opening address. Dr Lloyd-Jones was always on the look-out for men who had a special burden for revival and if he could get someone to speak who had personal experience of the phenomenon he would not miss the opportunity. One such speaker I recall clearly was David Davies. We had an outstanding day when Davies spoke of the great revival which he had seen in the Belgian Congo prior to the civil war and the change of name to Zaire. He began by saying that he had not come to tell us how to obtain revival, he would simply give us his own experience. In the area of the Congo where he was serving, the work and witness of the mission had been maintained over many years but some of the workers came to feel the need for greater evidence of the power of the Spirit of God in their midst. Accordingly they set aside times for earnest prayer for an outpouring of the Spirit. After some time there were the first appearances of change when a small group of local people came under conviction of sin.

The major change, however, first began in another area of the same mission where Davies' brother was serving. When his brother wrote to him with news of this, and of the extraordinary blessing which they were seeing, Davies replied cautiously and even reprimanded his brother for using extravagant language. Word came back, 'When the revival reaches you, you will use the same language!' So it was to prove. One night at the close of a service, an awesome sense of the presence of God and of His holiness, descended upon the whole congregation and people cried out in deep conviction. In the days which followed there were unusual manifestations of the power of God, as often occurs at such seasons, but these were not encouraged. The missionaries felt that they had to stand by and witness, and commit the whole work to God. Although they had sought to serve God faithfully for years, they also were *deeply* searched and convicted. Moral transformation took place in communities. Sins unknown before were brought to light with solemn repentance. The stealing of tools and other goods from government overseers had been widespread and the return of such items was now of such a scale that the authorities themselves were embarrassed. Even those with no previous sympathy for evangelical Christianity gave testimony to the change. Thus when one of the sisters of a local Roman Catholic convent was asked, 'What do you make of what is happening?' she replied, 'What you see is what happened in Acts 2.'

For me this whole day was thrilling. I think the words of Davies which impressed me most were, 'I can only describe it as God coming down among His people'. What happened was undoubtedly a preparation for the terrible persecution and bloodshed that was to follow a few years after the revival. Our speaker testified that most of those converted during this season of refreshing from the Lord stood firm through the later ordeal.

Before I turn from Westminster Chapel and Dr Lloyd-Jones I must also mention the other meetings I began attending there at this same time – the two-day Puritan Conference of which he was also the chairman. This annual event in December was open to all and the lecture hall was usually full. Six addresses would be given, followed by lively discussion. The great purpose was to acquaint a new generation with the spiritual riches of the Reformation and Puritan eras. The strange fact was that, while the names of such men as Calvin were well-known and revered in the tradition to which I belonged, their actual writings were seldom thoroughly studied or understood.

Along with calling my attention to the need of revival,

Dr Lloyd-Jones, and others at the Puritan Conference, thus made me think about history as I had not done before. It became clearer to me how restricted I had been in my thinking and reading. I knew a new burden for the success of the Gospel. I also saw the importance and blessedness of being with brethren who, though differing on some lesser matters, belonged together in Christ.

Side by side with the change which I knew through the new circle of friends at Westminster, was the influence of another 'friend' who I can say began to live with me from the early 1960s. Of course, I knew of the name of Spurgeon long before I heard of Dr Lloyd-Jones. I had purchased his book, *Unto the Uppermost*, containing twelve of his sermons, in the 1930s. But far from appreciating these sermons, I was really quite critical. In my Hyper-Calvinistic circles, the pastor of the Metropolitan Tabernacle, who had died in 1892, was generally considered an Arminian (Dr Lloyd-Jones' experience in that regard was not unique). I compared Spurgeon with J. C. Philpot, whose experimental writings on the struggles of the soul were our staple diet, and he seemed to be deficient as well as too flowery. I believe we felt we could only be sober if we were sombre. When a Gospel Standard writer produced *The Story of the Gospel in England* it contained no reference to C. H. Spurgeon.[1]

My re-introduction to Spurgeon came many years later, just before I began my pastorate at Jireh Chapel. One Sunday I was supplying the pulpit of the Gospel Standard chapel in Canterbury, whose pastor, Mr Denyer, was recently deceased. Mrs Denyer kindly told me that I would

[1] S. F. Paul, *The Story of the Gospel in England* (Ilfracombe: A. H. Stockwell, 1950).

be welcome to some of her husband's books and among those which I thus acquired was Spurgeon's *Evening by Evening* readings. These I began to use and to appreciate. Some time afterwards I had to give up the book in memorable circumstances. Mrs Denyer had come to stay with us and in the course of an evening I read Spurgeon's evening portion for that day aloud. Having done so, I asked her, 'Do you know whose writing that is?' She exclaimed in no uncertain terms, 'That is not my book, is it?' When I reminded her that it was among the books she had given me, she said that she had since looked for it everywhere. It had been given to them by a Scots minister and they had specially treasured it. Of course, I returned it to her at once.

Some time later, I was visiting a friend of Mrs Denyer's at Cranbrook and mentioned the above incident in passing. There was a gentleman from Northampton staying with her, and he immediately said, 'Would you like another copy? Thirty years ago, the book was a great blessing to me, and I vowed that I would give a copy to anyone that would accept one.' So I soon became the possessor for the second time of the book which has been my daily companion ever since. It was through its pages that I first began to love Spurgeon.

This episode is a reminder of something else which I slowly discovered. Charles Haddon Spurgeon was more widely used and admired in our circles than anyone would have suspected. Once a year I would preach for the late Stanley Delves of Crowborough. On those occasions I would use his study and it was evident that among the books he most used were many by Spurgeon. He told me that once he had agreed with everything he read in Philpot's sermons, but that when his reading had widened, Philpot had fallen into his rightful place. One of Spurgeon's deacons, William Olney Jr, had once visited Mr Delves while recovering from an illness. 'What was so remarkable about Spurgeon's ministry?' the pastor asked the visitor. 'I cannot tell you,' Olney replied, 'but once you heard him you never forgot it.'

On my last visit to my esteemed friend, George Rose, then in his nineties, when I mentioned Spurgeon, he replied, 'Bernard, C. H. Spurgeon was the greatest preacher of the last century.' Both Stanley Delves and George Rose were widely accepted and used in Gospel Standard churches. I believe Spurgeon's ministry had an influence on their own preaching but I came to regret that neither gave more public testimony to the help God had made him to them.

The book I first had from Mr Denyer's library was certainly a milestone in my life and soon I began to purchase everything I could find of Spurgeon's writings. In time I acquired most of the volumes of the *Metropolitan Tabernacle Pulpit* where most that is best in the Puritans can readily be found. I remember the profound effect the volumes of his biography by G. Holden Pike had on me. They stirred my spirit, and gave me a longing to be used of God more and more for the conversion of sinners. A concern for all people breathed in his words and the very spirit which moved him seemed to affect me as I read. *The Soul-Winner* was not merely the title of one of his books. It was his life. I recall how this struck me as I read one of his sermons on the marriage feast. At the end he uses every possible means to move his hearers, warning, pleading, persuading, cajoling, threatening and wooing.

I gained the same impression from an aunt of mine who

had heard Spurgeon and related her experience to me. Her father was the deacon of the Gospel Standard church in Clapham and owned a baker's shop facing the Common. At one time Spurgeon had lived close by and it was actually through his help that this church had ever been built. A builder had begun the work but for some reason could not continue. Spurgeon heard about it and procured the means for it to be completed. My aunt's father used to go to hear Spurgeon on Thursday evenings sometimes and one day, when she was perhaps six years old, he asked her, 'Heppie, would you like to go with me to the tabernacle tonight?' She went and never forgot the effect it had on her. The evening was very wet. During the service four white men and two coloured were to be baptised. The first thing Spurgeon said on coming to the rostrum was: 'Friends, you may wonder why the weather should be so inclement on such an occasion as this. It may well be that the inclemency of the weather has driven some in here tonight that would not otherwise have been here. Let us pray that God will meet with them and save them.'

Oh, that we might see the same earnestness in prayer for the lost in our day! I believe Spurgeon's praying was as effectual as his preaching. I have the two volumes of his prayers and even as you read they lift you up into the heavenlies and fill your soul with joy, praise and adoration, opening something of the glories that we shall yet see in the face of our dear Redeemer. I believe Spurgeon's success cannot be understood apart from his deep communion with the Lord. Prayer seemed to be natural to him. His life convinced me that if we are to see blessing and revival, we must get on our knees.

My new-found love and esteem for Spurgeon made me

want to visit the places of interest in his life. I went to Kelvedon, Essex, and saw the house where he was born which still stands today in the main street and bears a commemoration plaque. I made my first visit to Stambourne while I was still at Jireh, driven there by the kindness of one of my members. But being a staunch Gospel Standard man my friend had no interest in the place which Spurgeon knew so well during his years with his grandparents. A new chapel had been built but I believe it was the original pulpit. Close by I found his Aunt Ann's grave. The arbour was still there where Richard Knill took the young boy out early in the morning to talk with him and to marvel at his knowledge. I also saw the grass walk behind the arbour where his grandfather would meditate over his sermons. Ten years later, to my grief, when I went there again with my wife, I found that much had changed, with a large part of the old manse garden sold off for building plots. On that second visit it was cowslip time in the lanes of Essex. Spurgeon comments on how cowslips lined the road as he would go to tea at the local vicar's home with his grandfather. They were still there and it came home to me with sweetness that, while so much had gone, creation abides to witness to His gracious care. I have often given thanks that God's covenant with the earth is unconditional.

Another memorable visit was to Isleham and the River Lark where Spurgeon was baptised. When my friend, David Bugden, was pastor at Warboys, I mentioned to him my desire to visit the spot. He arranged for me to spend the night with him and the next day took me to the sacred spot – an experience I will never forget. I remembered the fears which the fifteen-year-old felt beforehand, and how, as he was immersed in that flood according to the command of the Lord, they all left him – 'the fish must have eaten them,' he later supposed, 'for they have never troubled me since!' Another pilgrimage to Waterbeach left me disappointed. There is a more modern chapel claiming some connection but nothing of real interest.

Spurgeon gave me a new desire to exalt a precious Christ. Gradually there were new notes in my preaching although my hearers may not have known the source. Twice while I was at Jireh I read one of Spurgeon's morning portions. The first time was on a Sunday which fell on 5 November and his reading spoke of God's wonderful goodness to us as a nation. That was an acceptable subject. But the next time his reading was based on the text, 'The harvest is past, the summer is ended and we are not saved.' From these words he pleaded with sinners and, after pointing out all their privileges and the swift passage of time, he added, 'Let me ask you, *will you ever be saved? Is there any likelihood of it?*' This was too much for some of my hearers who came to my vestry to complain that this was not in line with my preaching. It seemed obvious to them that the quotation was near to implying 'creature power and free will'. Perhaps I did not then myself fully realise the implications of what I was reading for I was still emerging from a long avoidance of anything like pleading with hearers to repent and trust in Christ. Only slowly did it come home to me that there was indeed a major contrast between the way the Gospel was presented in Spurgeon's congregation and in mine. Once, when I had been struck by the beseeching manner in which Spurgeon handled a text in one of his sermons, I read the text and some of his words to one of our old members and asked, 'If I were to preach from that text next Sunday, how would you have me handle it?' The response in severe tones was, 'I hope God would give you what to say'. 'But,' I replied, 'If I preached like that would you accept it?' Events which followed gave the answer to that question.

I acknowledge that no man is perfect but I am free to admit that Spurgeon became my example and hero in all the years that followed. I believe that, under God, we may have a hero but not an idol! (I am also thankful that God blesses many ministries if they are faithful and He does not have to raise up great men). Dr Lloyd-Jones was in many ways different from the Baptist leader yet he became to many of us at this time a living example of the same heritage which we were discovering in Spurgeon. It was a remarkable providence that the influence of the two men coalesced at this period, and that Spurgeon's voice spoke to minds and hearts in a manner which it had not done since his death. His words were coming true, 'I am quite willing to be eaten by dogs for the next fifty years but the more distant future shall vindicate me.'

In the 1950s and 60s there was a recovering of truth in England yet the voices which swayed our hearts taught us to work and pray for a blessing and reviving which would touch the lives of nations. It may sometimes seem that those who are not preachers cannot do much but the effects of prayer are beyond all calculation, and who can say what the passing on of books, such as the one which Mrs Denyer 'accidentally' gave to me, may do? Certainly, one practical effect of what happened to me at this time was that I began the habit of giving books to friends and church officers, even though they might not always be valued at the time. And henceforth, whenever I married a couple, I always gave them a presentation copy of Spurgeon's *Morning by Morning* or his *Evening by Evening*. I believe this was a means of bringing some to a more balanced understanding of the Gospel. The truth of God, spoken or written, has not lost its power. I close this chapter with an anonymous testimony to Spurgeon's sermons to which I can add my Amen:

Mr Spurgeon's 'Sermons' have brought a heavenly atmosphere around me and have been to my poor dusty heart as the dew. They have laid hold of me as with hooks of steel, and have kept me from falling, and fastened me permanently to the grand old doctrines of the Puritans. They have made me gentle, hopeful, forgiving, patient. They have stirred me like a clarion call, and rallied all my powers, and made me like a war horse, ready for the fight. They have opened up before me new beauty in the Word, made Christ more real and precious, filled my heart with an intense love to Him, and made me more anxious to do good to men, and glorify His holy name. When my home has been shadowed by sickness, darkness and death, I have taken down the volumes, and read until my heart has grown calm, and I could say, 'Father, not my will, but Thine, be done.'

8

The Error of Hyper-Calvinism

Readers will remember that I was brought up with Gospel Standard folk and was closely involved with them in my ministry. I still feel great affection for them. It will be as well at this point to sketch their history in a little more detail, as this will explain why we had to part company.

One whom these friends rightly hold in high esteem is the godly J. C. Philpot, who was for many years the editor of their magazine, the *Gospel Standard*. An eminent Greek and Hebrew scholar, he might well have become a Church of England bishop. He seceded, however, when he saw the evil of having men in the ministry who, though learned, were nevertheless unregenerate. He often said that he would rather listen to the preaching of a ploughman than to that of a doctor of divinity who was devoid of grace, *i.e.* unconverted. Unfortunately, what happened was that many of his admirers in the GS churches had neither gifts nor education, but took his statement about ploughmen almost literally. Some actually despised natural learning or formal training, and condemned the use of commentaries. The sad result was that ministers often preached their own experience without any attempt at exposition or practical application. This left congregations in a subjective rut. Experience is, of course, vital, but we must have balance – and that means preaching the whole counsel of God.

This situation was compounded in the 1930s when a movement arose which deeply disturbed the GS group of churches. Called 'the God-honouring Movement', it was set on foot by a Mr F. Foster, pastor of their church in Patricroft, and was taken up by J. K. Popham in his New Year Address to the *Gospel Standard*, 1934. The whole intention was to restrict their ministers to preaching only in GS churches, and to walk separately from all other Strict Baptist churches. Their ministers had to sign a form to this end. I well remember my father asking the visiting ministers, 'Have you signed up?' The following publicly protested: S. Delves, George Rose, E. A. Brooker, E. G. Rowell – and they were supported by others. These godly men contended that it was not *where* you preached, but *what* you preached that mattered. They were publicly labelled dissidents and recalcitrants.

This movement not only did a lot of damage, but was in absolute opposition to the plain command of our Lord, who declared, 'Go into all the world and preach the gospel to every creature'. In writing to a friend afterwards, J. K. Popham said, 'I fell in with the strong assertion without a thought or prayer. Seeking the Lord should have been first. Oh, my folly and sin'. And again later, 'My conscience made me sorry to have taken up what should have been left in the hand of God'.[1] Sadly, in a new edition of this *Memoir*, a foreword by J. Broome still uses the same description of those who do not accept the movement.

[1] John H. Gosden, *Memoir and Letters of James Kidwell Popham* (London: Farncombe & Sons, 1938), pp. 236–37.

The failure to 'preach the gospel to every creature' leads us to a consideration of what has become known historically as Hyper-Calvinism, which was the main cause of division at Jireh.

As regards definition of the term I cannot do better than quote Dr Martyn Lloyd-Jones:

A Hyper-Calvinist is one who says that the offer of salvation is only made to the redeemed, and that no preacher of the gospel should preach Christ and offer salvation to all and sundry.

The great majority of Bible believers have never doubted that it is their joy and privilege to urge anyone and everyone everywhere to repent and believe the gospel. They see no problem here. The 'problem' is in the minds of Hyper-Calvinists, who argue that if God is sovereign (which He is) and has decreed to save only the elect (which He has), and if man is dead in trespasses and sins and therefore totally incapable of repentance and faith (which he is), then it is absurd to offer God's salvation to him.

Logically considered, this type of argumentation is watertight. We are not, however, dealing with fallen human logic but with God's revelation. The Bible teaches both divine sovereignty and human responsibility, and we are to hold both elements of this paradox in balance, even though we cannot reconcile them. The Hyper-Calvinist, while rightly teaching God's eternal decree and human inability, denies man's responsibility. But human inability to do anything spiritual is a *sinful* inability and it in no way abrogates our responsibility.

As in all matters of faith and practice, the Scripture is our guide – and the evidence is overwhelming. Thus, in Isaiah

45:22 (Spurgeon's conversion verse), God calls to sinners everywhere: 'Look unto me, and be ye saved, all the ends of the earth'. Our Lord Himself commissions His apostles to go into the world and teach all nations (*Matt.* 28:19). We know that God commands all men everywhere to repent (*Acts* 17:30). Could anything be more universal in scope?

Some have sought to turn the thrust of this argument by casting doubt on God's willingness to save all. Let God answer this unworthy thought: 'I have no pleasure in the death of the wicked: but that the wicked turn from his way and live' (*Ezek.* 33:11). We are told quite explicitly that 'God is not willing that any should perish but that all should come to repentance' (*2 Pet.* 3:9). Our blessed Lord, while here on earth, loved the unrepentant Rich Young Ruler (*Mark* 10:21) and wept over a Jerusalem that spurned His proffered embrace (*Luke* 19:41–2; *Matt.* 23:37).

There can be no question but that some of the Articles of Faith of the Gospel Standard churches are Hyper-Calvinist in nature. It was the gradual realisation of this fact that changed the course of my life and transformed the church situation in Tenterden, as explained in the previous chapter.

I am happy to confirm that the major part of the Gospel Standard statement of faith is orthodox and to this part I adhere. It is in the denial of the free offer of the gospel that it deviates from Scripture. Thus Article 24 limits the gospel invitation to those under conviction of sin. Articles 26 and 29 deny that it is everyone's duty to repent and believe the gospel, so the gospel is not to be offered indiscriminately to all. Here we have the very essence of Hyper-Calvinism.

Normally, Bible-believing Christians are careful to base articles of faith on Scripture, but Articles 32–34, unlike the earlier Articles, are left totally without biblical verses in support! This is surely wrong. Yet GS churches are bound absolutely to them. Article 32 asserts that we should not use the book of Acts as our authority and model for gospel preaching whereas in fact that is precisely what we are to do. Articles 33 and 34 deny an open offer and also effectively deny human responsibility.[1]

These Articles are not only alien to the Scriptures and true Christianity but are also the antithesis of all that is best in evangelical Reformed tradition. Spurgeon had reason to say, 'The Calvinism of some men is not the Calvinism of John Calvin, nor the Calvinism of the Puritans, much less the Christianity of God.'[2] The logic on which the Gospel Standard articles object to preachers calling all men to faith received specific comment from Calvin himself when he wrote:

Some object that God would be inconsistent with himself, in inviting all without distinction while he elects only a few. Thus, according to them, the universality of the promise destroys the distinction of special grace. Some moderate men speak in this way, not so much for the purpose of suppressing truth, as to get quit of puzzling questions, and curb excessive curiosity. The intention is laudable, but the design is by no means to be approved.[3]

---

[1] The Gospel Standard Articles will be found in J. H. Gosden, *What Gospel Standard Baptists Believe* (Kington Langley: Gospel Standard Societies, 1993).

On this subject see also *My Life and Books: The Reminiscences of S. M. Houghton* (Edinburgh: Banner of Truth, 1988), pp. 29–33; Iain H. Murray, *The Life of Arthur W. Pink* (Edinburgh: Banner of Truth, 1981), pp. 47–62, 143–49.

[2] *New Park Street Pulpit*, vol. 5 (London, 1860), p. 367–68.

[3] *Institutes of the Christian Religion*, Henry Beveridge (James Clarke: London, 1949), vol. 2, p. 221.

Similarly the reformer wrote in other places:

God invites all indiscriminately to salvation... The gate of salvation is set open to all men; neither is there any other thing which keepeth us back from entering in, save only our own unbelief ... Though it is offered to all for salvation, it does not yield this fruit in any but the elect... God ... shows himself to be reconciled to the whole world, when he invites all men without exception to faith in Christ.[1]

By claiming that the promise of salvation in Christ cannot be addressed to all men, Hyper-Calvinism has to present another means by which individuals may know if the promise is addressed to them. This it does by encouraging preachers to describe feelings and experiences by which an individual, looking at himself, may discover if God has begun a work in his life. Thus there developed the type of 'experimental preaching' favoured in these circles, the purpose of which was to help individuals to discover a

---

[1] See the Calvin Translation Society vols, *Synoptic Gospels,* 1, p. 116; *Acts,* 1, p. 92; *Synoptic Gospels,* 2, p. 257; *John,* 1, p. 125. Quoted in J. Graham Miller, *Calvin's Wisdom* (Edinburgh: Banner of Truth, 1992, p. 119). Andrew Fuller wrote to a man of Hyper-Calvinistic views: 'Were you to read many of Calvin's sermons, without knowing who was the author, you would be led, from the views you appear at present to entertain, to pronounce him an Arminian; neither would Goodwin, nor Owen, nor Charnock, nor Flavel, nor Bunyan, escape the charge. These men believed and preached the doctrines of grace; but not in such a way as to exclude exhortations to the unconverted to repent and believe in Jesus Christ.' *Complete Works of A. Fuller* (London, 1841), p. 889. J. C. Philpot not only denied the legitimacy of exhortations being addressed to unbelievers but is on record disapproving of exhortations being addressed to Christians on the grounds that they are no 'more able to perform spiritual actions than natural men, unless the Lord work in them to will and to do of his good pleasure.' *Gospel Standard,* 1841, p. 82. Conditions of spiritual inertia were bound to follow such teaching.

life-giving work of the Spirit in their hearts *before* they believe they are able to rest on the promises of the Gospel.

The effect of this is to reverse the way in which sinners are to be brought to peace. As Professor John Murray has written:

We entrust ourselves to Christ not because we believe we have been saved but as lost sinners in order that we may be saved. It is to us in our lost condition that the warrant of faith is given. [1]

The warrant of faith is, therefore, the full, free, and un-restricted overture of Christ in the gospel. This overture is not simply the warrant for believing in Christ for salvation. It places upon every one confronted with it the demand for repentance towards God and faith towards the Lord Jesus Christ, and it offers insult to the grace and faithfulness of God to require more as the warrant for faith. To interpose the necessity of additional information or of some precedent, saving experience to assure us of God's grace is to impugn the veracity of God's promises in the gospel. For a sinner to plead that it is presumptuous to believe in Christ for salvation until he receives some individual experiential assurance of Christ's willingness to receive him is to distrust the word of the Saviour in the free overtures of his grace. [2]

Where such a serious change in the presentation of the Gospel occurs, it is bound to result in evangelistic decline. The churches, instead of believing that the Gospel message has relevance and urgency for all men, begin to concern themselves chiefly with looking for marks of grace within their own circle. I often saw examples of this and I will cite a few.

[1] *Redemption: Accomplished and Applied* (Edinburgh: Banner of Truth, 1979), pp. 109–10.
[2] *Collected Writings of John Murray* (Edinburgh: Banner of Truth, 1977), vol. 2, p. 257.

Years ago, I was having tea after preaching in a GS chapel in the West Country, when a lady from another GS church said, 'Last Sunday we had two young people come in. They did not look like our sort and they went out before the sermon. I was glad to see them go!'

In another case a young man drove his father to preach in a GS chapel which they had difficulty in locating. At lunch-time he said to the deacon, 'Would it not be better to have a notice-board?' The reply came back, 'Oh no, we don't want the world in!'.

At the last anniversary services at Jireh, whilst I was pastor, the chapel was packed, with some sitting in the vestry. When this was mentioned to one of the deacons, his reply was, 'We are getting the wrong kind of people' – they were not all GS folk.

But this kind of teaching, as well as failing to reach those without, does serious damage within. With the elimination of all calls for faith and repentance, and the disappearance of the biblical emphasis on duty, hearers can all too easily be led to suppose that conversion has nothing to do with themselves. Year after year such hearers can be found always in the same condition, 'waiting' for some change which they may confess they need but are never any nearer to obtaining.

I recall one illustration of this, out of many I could recount. A lady moved into our town some years ago and asked to see me. She continued to attend a church some miles away where the ministry and outlook was Hyper-Calvinistic. Whenever I visited her, over some length of time, I was always welcome but I ever found her sad. She was always in the same spiritual state, complaining of her sinfulness, and doubting if she was 'a child of God', and

[87]

whether she had ever been 'called by grace'. Occasionally, as we spoke, her hopes might seem to rise but she would soon return to her former position. I think if I had said, 'I do not believe you are a Christian,' she would have been very upset.

I do not doubt that there is real spiritual danger in this wrong emphasis on inability. Spurgeon saw it in his day when, referring to the effect of 'ultra-Calvinistic' doctrines, he wrote:

Griffiths says that travellers in Turkey carry with them lozenges of opium, on which is stamped *mash Allah*, the gift of God. Too many sermons are just such lozenges. Grace is preached but duty denied. Divine predestination is cried up but human responsibility is rejected. Such teaching ought to be shunned as poisonous, but those who by reason of use have grown accustomed to the sedative, condemn all other preaching, and cry up their opium lozenges of high doctrine as *the truth*, the precious gift of God. It is to be feared that this poppy-juice doctrine has sent many souls to sleep who will wake up in hell.[1]

Upon true believers this kind of teaching has a different effect. By its tendency to rob Christians of the comfort and enjoyment of the Christian life, it hinders them from giving the honour and praise to God which is His due. Although we may all pass through seasons of darkness, temptation and uncertainty, surely we cannot really doubt what God has done for all who trust in Him. There should always be a resting upon the Word of God and His promises. Those who are constantly looking within their own hearts are always likely to be in a state of uncertainty, for feelings constantly change. The godly Robert Murray M'Cheyne

[1] C. H. Spurgeon, *Feathers for Arrows* (London, 1870), p. 65.

used to say, 'For every look at self, take ten looks at Christ!' To be constantly doubting what God has done and promised, when He is the unchanging, faithful, gracious and loving Saviour, must surely be grieving to Him.

Where this teaching prevails witness is likely to be very ineffective. We are commanded to be the Lord's witnesses, but how can we witness confidently and convincingly if we doubt our own salvation? Maybe this is why people in Hyper-Calvinistic churches do not commonly witness to those around them; indeed, I know from experience that many actually speak against witnessing to the world. Their beliefs have led them to an unscriptural separation and withdrawal from society. That cannot be right in the light of our Lord's teaching and example.

Some of us were led away by Hyper-Calvinism partly because it is teaching which takes the Bible seriously. Certainly we must all hold all that Scripture teaches, including divine sovereignty in election and regeneration. But to deduce from such beliefs what the Bible does not teach can be as injurious as actually denying the truth. May these words prove a warning to some who may be inclined to this error.

9

Two Special Friends

I have written earlier of two well-known figures whose ministry contributed much to the change in my thought and ministry. But our lives are made up of many influences and before I finish these pages I want to pay tribute to two much-loved friends to whom I came to owe much. Unknown, perhaps, to the Christian world at large, yet they both brought a blessing to a number of us which will not be forgotten.

To the first, Ebenezer John Knight, I have already referred in passing. When I first came to know him he was living in Wiltshire, in the west of England, where he had been preaching for many years among Gospel Standard churches. In 1960 the outward course of his life was suddenly changed by a call to the pastorate of Zion Gospel Standard Strict Baptist Chapel in Grand Rapids, Michigan. He believed this was of God and parted from us with that assurance. On his first visit back to England in 1962 he spoke for me at Jireh Chapel and in that address told us of how he had been led across the Atlantic. He also gave us the background of the situation in Grand Rapids, together with some of his experiences since his arrival. Two hundred people heard him on that occasion. We were moved and the address was printed. Like myself, 'Eb' Knight had grown up in the doctrine and outlook of the Gospel Standard churches and to all appearances that was where he would remain. So strict indeed was he in background that on one occasion when he heard a brother address God in public prayer as 'Our Father' he felt compelled to remonstrate with him.

But a change was at hand greater than the 3,000 miles he had travelled to Michigan. How precisely it began I do not know. Eb had occasionally attended Westminster Chapel before he left for the United States and probably some questions were already arising in his mind at that date. He must have noticed that Dr Lloyd-Jones did not 'trim' and qualify gospel texts which had a universal note about them as he himself had been in the habit of doing. Slowly he came to see that the type of gospel preaching to which he was accustomed was closely connected with religious conditions in which doubt in God's promises was almost treated as healthy. A situation had developed in which assurance of salvation was commonly regarded as though it were presumption. This was true not only in his circle in Grand Rapids but at Jireh where I still ministered at that time. When a young woman under his ministry had been sweetly blessed with full assurance, she wrote to one of my deacons relating her experience. His comment to me was, 'If she had said, "I hope", I could have accepted it.' Eb wrote to me of encouragement he saw among some of the young in his congregation and of the contrast between them and older members who 'have been taught more or less to doubt their standing in Christ, and they look with the greatest suspicion on any semblance of assurance.'

As my friend's eyes began to open to the situation, it

seemed worse to him than what he had left behind in England. Speaking of a neighbouring congregation, he wrote to me at one point:

In the Netherlands Reformed Church here, they are plainly told that their safest place is to be 'in prison', doubting. They make a virtue of their unbelief; it is their religion. Be thankful when you feel you have nothing; when you have something, then doubt the reality of it to be safe! You really have to be in things over here to appreciate the terrible nature of what has sprung out of an unbalanced holding of the truth. By the way, when folk say, 'Without me ye can do nothing,' they little realise what they are saying. The word literally means, 'Severed from me ye can do nothing.' Well, who are those severed from Christ? God's people? Never! They are indissolubly united to Christ … the word which belongs to God's dear people is, 'I can do all things through Christ that strengthens me'.

In what order his convictions began to change I am not sure but I recall the impression which one reprint made on him. It helped him to see how older preachers – as the gospel minister described by John Bunyan – *pleaded* with men. Whereas he would once have regarded any appeals to sinners to trust in Christ as unsound, he now had serious misgivings. As he wrote to me:

If ever we felt warmed up as Whitefield and Spurgeon did in their day, then we should doubtless depart from our phraseology. I greatly fear that as a denomination in our efforts to avoid error, we have missed much of the truth. There are many things among us today which grieve me and give me cause for much searching of heart. I will not dogmatise, but take the following case. There has been published a book of Whitefield's early sermons – five or six of them.[1] A deacon of the Gospel Standard Committee read

---

[1] *Select Sermons of George Whitefield* (London: Banner of Truth, 1959).

them and made the remark, 'They are not fit to read in our pulpits today.' What struck me forcibly was that there were more genuine conversions under one of the sermons of Whitefield than there have been under all the many sermons preached by Gospel Standard ministers in the whole century since; yet they are called sermons not suitable to read today! Every fair-minded person will have to admit that the wrong is among us some-where. I, with others, try to make various excuses but I fear we are wriggling from the truth.

Almost all our contact was by letter and in part because we were both being led in the same kind of path there developed a deep brotherly love between us. One summer, after relating his weariness in temperatures around one hundred degrees Fahrenheit, he continued:

I am thankful you feel free to write to me as you do. Although we do not want to spend precious time writing about unprofitable things, that need not hinder us from unburdening our hearts and cases to one another. Your letters to me are like a breath of English air, and I cannot express to you the pleasure they bring to one brother in this far-off land. Post arrives here about 12 p.m. – our dinner time; it is invariably a very long dinner-time when such letters as yours arrive. This is not surprising when you think of the roots we have left over in England – family, brethren and the churches where we ministered for over twenty-five years.

I have already mentioned how at this period I was being guided into a more careful sermon preparation, with the use of notes. Eb was having the same experience. He had come to see that the idea that God gives preachers their material directly, perhaps even as they enter a pulpit, was responsible for many sermons being 'a mere irksome series of unprofitable repetitions'. True preaching involved much work beforehand, including study:

We have to receive before we can give, and if there is no reading, meditation, prayer, waiting on the Lord, and passing through trial, exercise and temptation, being supported under them, there will be nothing as it were, laid up in the heart, to come out of the mouth. It is this want of reading, meditation and spiritual exercise that makes the ministry of the day so lean, and to wear out so soon ... I may have over-emphasised my point, and, my brother, what is more, I do not speak as if you need such advice more than I do; but reading your exercises and desires, I find they come very near to my own, and we will try to help each other along the road.

As in my own case, however, it was not so much the change in his preparation for the pulpit as it was the change in his content which led to trouble. In a letter of 1965 he wrote:

I preached two sermons yesterday from Isaiah 45:22. In the morning, I paved the way for what I anticipated would be called by some a 'nearly free-will sermon'. However, my morning preparation takes the ground from under their feet somewhat. Bernard, I cannot preach anyhow else. Florrie [his wife] tells me plainly that I did not preach like this before in England. I may humbly say that I am conscious of the hand of the Lord upon me, in my own experience and I know more of that rest in faith and of the beauty, fullness and firmness of the Gospel than I ever did before. I feel at liberty, not only in warning sinners, but in pleading with them. As C. H. Spurgeon said, 'We want labourers, not loiterers'.

On the same subject he wrote again later:

You will be interested to know that I have had the liberty to preach from some texts which I have always avoided through fear of 'free-will'. John 3:16 is one of them. Upon reflection, I ought to be ashamed of myself as a professing Gospel minister that, as far as I can remember, I have never before preached from it. It ought to be the very sum and substance of our ministry. Then there are two others – John 7:37 ('If any man thirst, let him come unto me and drink'), and John 12:32 ('And I, if I be lifted up, will draw all men unto me'). My wife, of course, knowing my past ministry, anxiously and prayerfully followed recent developments, but not without many a wriggle in her seat at what might come out next.

He went on to speak of how the conviction that there are no hopeless cases under the gospel was affecting his ministry and of how he knew a new yearning for people and for their salvation. But despite the care which he took to bring his people along with him, he found, as I did, that trouble was unavoidable. It was at this time that I was reaching my own crisis at Jireh Chapel. To a letter in which I told him something of it, he replied:

I had a great urge to sit down and answer you immediately but circumstances would not permit. But I did bow my head before the Lord our God and try to pour out my heart before Him in petition in your behalf. It is indeed a remarkable thing that we are found walking in much the same pathway. There are many differences in our relative positions; different problems, different kinds of opposition and different methods employed by our opposers, but we are on common ground in finding opposition to the particular line of truth in which I believe the Lord is leading us both . . .

Brother, you are being called upon to walk more closely with your Lord and Master; with Him it culminated in His being spat upon and crucified. Look unto Him to help you and uphold you. I know He will not fail you, nor forsake you in the warfare to which He has called you. Endure hardness as a good soldier of Jesus Christ. The scourge of tongue, especially from your saints, is not easy to bear, but His grace is sufficient! It will be no burden for us to remember you continually in our prayers, that He will bless you, make you a blessing to His Church, not counting the cost, bearing you up under the reproach and the shame. Still go on, preaching the Word in season and out of season, with your eyes fixed on Jesus, and with a single eye to His honour and glory. I have not experienced any hostility as you have. I am in the midst of a more theological battle and I could not begin to tell you in writing; one would have to come here and experience it first hand.

In Eb's case the controversy eventually led to a secession of some twenty-five older members from his congregation. It proved to be no great blow to him for greater liberty followed and a number of instances of God's wondrous saving grace and power, especially among the young people. On his first arrival in 1960 he had been told of the special need among the young and it was amongst them that his ministry was especially used. Before he laid down the work there in 1976 there was at least one time of special blessing when twelve were baptised together. He and his wife then returned to England and to the West Country which they loved. His affection for the Gospel Standard people never left him and it was a sorrow to him to have his name removed from the list of GS ministers where it had been for thirty-five years. When he came to speak for me at Trinity few of those who had heard him with such appreciation in 1962 would come to listen. Such things were painful for him. He longed to see brethren show a more Christlike spirit and to possess a willingness to understand and unite with other Christians.

In his latter years his health was failing but he was still preaching a little in the Spring of 1990. On his homecall at the end of that year, I lost a dear brother with whom I had long walked in the closest fellowship and union in Christ.

His funeral was on 4 January 1991 and I will never forget the singing of the doxology at his graveside in Colerne churchyard.

*   *   *

Associated in my mind and heart with Ebenezer Knight is another special friend though in some ways they were very different. The truth is that there were things about Hector Ryland Brooke which would have made him different from anyone. As his middle name may suggest, he was born into a family with a long Baptist tradition. It was a Ryland who baptised William Carey in the eighteenth century. His godly father was one of a large family which came from Sodbury in Gloucestershire but he had moved to the area of Bath by the time that Hector was born in 1900. The Ryland name actually came from Pastor J. R. Huntley of Widcombe Chapel, Bath, whom his father much admired. The father was only forty-four (and Hector twelve) when he died as the result of a bicycle accident. So I never knew him, but I remember two of his brothers who both held pastorates in Strict Baptist churches. Walter was at West Street Chapel, Croydon, then a large congregation. I heard him preach a number of times, and he also assisted at my elder sister's wedding. Arthur exercised ministries at Coventry and Hailsham before returning to Bath.

Hector Brooke first joined the civil service on leaving school. Always adventurous, he left that work in 1921 and by the next year was in Cuba where he worked with the Fyffe Banana Company until about 1926. I think he believed that he had come to know the Saviour at an early age but, if that was so, this time in his life must be described as one of serious backsliding. 'However I escaped utter ruin I do not know,' he later wrote. 'I gambled, I drank, I desecrated the Lord's Day in horse racing, in pig hunting, in cinema attendances . . . Yet I was always conscious of God and even in the midst of such revellings my memory would suddenly conjure up a scene of my boyhood days.' Home again in England, he returned to better influences, staying with his uncle Walter in Croydon. It was through Walter Brooke that he came to know Grace ('Greeba') Newnham whom he married in 1935. The next year, humbled through serious business difficulties, they both confessed their faith and were baptised. Subsequently they were successful in the drapery business, first in London and, from 1950, in Malvern where they remained until his retirement in 1965. Soon after that date he and Grace returned to live in the scenes of his childhood, buying a house at Batheaston.

Hector's wife and myself came from the same part of the country and had gone to school together. Thereafter we lost touch until the 1960s when one of Grace's sisters saw a letter I had written to a local paper on some subject and had sent it to Grace who then wrote to me. The outcome was that I promised to visit them when next on a preaching tour in the West Country. This I did in April 1964, renewing our acquaintance after more than thirty years, and forming a friendship with Hector which grew deeper with every succeeding visit. Their home in Batheaston became mine whenever I was in the West Country. Grace was a beautiful hostess in more ways than one. Together they enjoyed entertaining many Christians and especially those who were in any way connected with the resurgence of free-grace beliefs that was then in evidence in England. The republishing work of the Banner of Truth Trust and of other publishers, filled him with joy, and no one was a greater enthusiast than he for good books and good preaching. While no pastor himself, he surely filled that role to not a few of us who were.

It was not until the 1960s that Hector finally broke with Hyper-Calvinism and with chapels where it was still supported. His experience ran parallel to that of Eb Knight's (whom he also knew as a friend) and my own, but he was ahead of us in his catholicity of spirit, having profited from the ministry of Dr Campbell Morgan and others outside Gospel Standard circles as far back as the 1930s. Referring to that earlier date, he recalled his disappointment on the first occasion at Westminster Chapel that he found a young Welshman, Martyn Lloyd-Jones, in the place of Morgan. The feeling was short-lived and he prized the preaching at Westminster Chapel long before most in our circle had ever heard of it.[1]

While his doctrinal convictions finally settled decisively in the tradition of Whitefield, William Jay and Spurgeon, he was ready to learn from all Christians and deplored narrowness wherever he found it. When I told him in a letter of a recent addition to Trinity from the Salvation Army, he replied:

I expect Pat Timms may have as much to teach you as you to teach her. And that would apply to me too. As sure as you attempt to tone down some theological beliefs, you may to that extent reduce enthusiasm as well as usefulness. You may give her more depth of doctrine, but is it depth of doctrine that woos a

[1] There is a letter of Dr Lloyd-Jones to him in the *Letters of D. Martyn Lloyd-Jones* (Edinburgh: Banner of Truth, 1994), pp. 87–88, and Iain H. Murray used an extract from his diary, describing a meeting at Westminster Chapel, in *David Martyn-Lloyd-Jones: The Fight of Faith* (Edinburgh: Banner of Truth, 1990), p. 191.

sinner to Christ? We are so apt to say that men such as Brengle have but little theology, but Brengle had enough to challenge 'the tongues movement' of his day and overcame it. Can we do this in our day?

In another letter he wrote to me in similar vein:

I have had some contact this week with a Pentecostal, and have been humbled by his true spirituality; his Saviour is so very real to him, yet I am bound to differ from him in some things theologically. I had to confess that there are many parts of God's Word that are largely untouched by me. He was constantly referring to the gifts of the Spirit, and speaking confidently of possessing them and their necessity in order to live the Christian life. Do you know, I have hardly considered them, neither do I remember hearing much preaching from the pulpit regarding them, except a side-remark made in a sort of semi-critical fashion. This man is a dental mechanic and is totally other-worldly. God uses him in conversions as he visits various national institutions, homes for the elderly, prisons etc. I believe we often feel a great union to each other in having a desire to love all who love the Lord Jesus Christ.

Another time he wrote, 'The Pentecostal people *expect* miracles after prayer. Is this the exercise of faith? I just *hope* after my prayer, is this why I seem to achieve so little?'

Nothing meant more to him than did the need for a recovery of powerful Gospel preaching and he did every-thing he could to encourage it. Once, while still at Malvern (where there was no living church), he felt so famished that on the spur of the moment he decided, 'We must go and hear some good preaching'. So he drove more than three hundred miles to Edinburgh! The importance of that visit, however, was probably not so much in the preaching he heard as it was in the news Professor G. N. M. Collins gave him of what God was doing in various parts of England and of which Hector was then unaware. Out of concern for a number of students in Malvern, he began to invite various reformed preachers to come and speak in their home so that they could hear some good ministry. Among the younger men whose ministry he prized was Pastor A. N. Martin whom he first met at Largs in 1969. Somewhat later, after listening to tapes by Martin, he wrote to me:

We have just got through Al Martin's Aberystwyth addresses on sanctification. They are truly great, though I need to hear them several times yet before I feel I have penetrated his thought. Not that he is difficult, but his matter is so extensive and so tremendously challenging. Yet our Gospel Standard minnows grow liverish at the very mention of progressive sanctification. After hearing this man on any given subject, he seems to invest it with paramount importance. In his last address, he pleaded with pastors present to give their hearers solid, systematic preaching, book by book, chapter by chapter . . . all Scripture is given by God and we need all.

Hector loved every preacher who spoke the truth and to his heart. Sometimes he had surprises as he reports at the close of one letter:

I could not finish this on Saturday night – too tired, but was greatly refreshed by the ministry on Sunday. All my prejudices, largely the result of C's stories about S. M. Houghton, were swept aside. His text was Proverbs 23:23, 'Buy the truth and sell it not'. He said time would not allow him to deal with both clauses, so he would confine his remarks to 'Buy the truth'. It was a powerful discourse. Succinct and to the point always, I was quite won over from the start. For an introduction he gave Bunyan's pilgrim at Vanity Fair. I thought it was much more to the point than endeavouring to explain 'buying'. I did not really expect to shake hands with him, but I had a grand time with him. Leslie was expected to preach at night. I said to them both, 'Surely this exposition cannot be left as it is, it must be completed'. Leslie agreed, so we had the remainder, 'and sell it not' at night.

It was this same enthusiasm for all that honoured Christ that made him so interested in scenes memorable for past events in church history. He would take visitors to such places as Tyndale's one-time home at Little Sodbury, and to the church where Hugh Latimer preached at West Kington. We and our wives once spent a week together at Carlton, near Bedford. We visited many places of interest in this Bunyan country, including the old church of John Berridge at Everton and another at Huntingdon. He loved the rich brown of the interiors of such old buildings which never appealed to me. (He was not enthusiastic when Grove Chapel, where he was married, changed its sombre interior to pale blue and white!) Much as he enjoyed those days in Bedfordshire I will never forget when he got in the car to go home. He was like a schoolboy jumping up and down in his seat, saying, 'Oh, we are going home!' He was a real home man, and once told me he felt it should be a punishable offence to make a man go away from home after he reached the age of seventy.

After his return to the Bath area, he worshipped in the little chapel at Bathford which he had attended as a boy. Originally opened by William Jay, it had fallen on hard times by the 1960s, having no pastor and no real leadership. For the rest of his days he regarded the support of that little work as a calling from God. Occasionally he preached there himself, regarding it as a high privilege and heavy responsibility. As in other things, his method of preparation was somewhat unique to himself. He wrote notes though he did not seem to use them in the pulpit. 'I would think,' his wife says, 'he almost knew them by heart, as often when he was missing for a length of time, if I looked out of the side window of the bedroom, I could see him, in the potting shed, preaching away for all his might to the stored apples and gardening stuff.'

I am sure he saw nothing humorous about that situation although a dry sense of humour was no small part of his make-up. I remember him telling me, on one occasion, of how he and Grace had spent a Saturday decorating the chapel at Bathford for the harvest service to please the few old people attending. On the next day, he added, 'There I was peering at the preacher between sprays of asparagus and having my eye on a big onion which I was hoping to take home after it was all over!'

He often wrote to me about the preaching of our day and I am sure he was right in his assessment of our main deficiency. As he wrote to me in 1976:

You know I fear we are more concerned about our doctrinal rectitude, than we are about really knowing Christ and being overwhelmed by his person, and having that degree of intimacy with Him which seems, Oh, so hard to achieve. 'That Christ may dwell in your hearts by faith . . . and to know the love of Christ which passeth knowledge.' It was this possession of Him in a real experimental way that enabled our forefathers so to preach him, as to reach men's hearts. Don't you think we often fail to get just there?[1]

[1] After his death, his diary showed how much this was on his heart. In one characteristic entry, after he had preached at Bathford, he wrote: 'Once again helped and upheld. But have I glorified Christ? have I so presented Him as to endear Him to all loving hearts, and to awaken a desire in others to know Him, and to some who have grown cold to move towards Him in confession of their sin? May it be so!'

I remember him telling me of a day of fasting that he kept. His wife was away, visiting her relatives, so he was alone. That morning he rose about 7 a.m. with a desire to fast. He made himself a cup of tea and retired to read and pray. He took up John's Gospel, would read a chapter and then spend time in prayer. Feeling something of the inditing of the Holy Spirit, he continued to read and pray until about 4 p.m. when, he said, his liberty seemed to cease. Very remarkably, he commented, there had been no caller at the door or on the phone the whole day. The effect on him was that the things of this life seemed of very little importance, and he felt quite weaned from them, with the matters of the soul and of eternity all-important. I believe this is true fasting! Who can tell the value of such devotion, and the power of prayer for those prayed for?

He also wrote to me of the conflicts which he experienced and he knew many such incidents as the following:

A few days ago, I went to bed and Satan assailed me sorely with a catalogue of all my past sins. I said, 'Lord, I have got a prickly pillow tonight, I do not want to die on such a pillow.' I felt too weak to exercise much faith, but my beloved Lord came to my rescue with His Word, 1 John 1:7–9. He did it all; I did not lift a finger, and I found rest and peace in Him and went to sleep like a little child. Then the next day I was in trouble again with the Doctor's last chapter. This book has been such a blessing to me, yet its last words, almost, plunged me into grief.[1] In effect, he says, 'The man who knows nothing about suffering for Christ is in a dreadful state.' You see, I have never suffered for Christ; you and Gwen have, and so has Pat, but not I, and so I was brought

[1] The reference is to D. Martyn Lloyd-Jones, *Romans: Exposition of Chapter 8:5–17* (Edinburgh: Banner of Truth, 1974), p. 437.

very low. Then again God's Word came to my rescue, 'The blood of Jesus Christ his Son cleanses us from all sin,' and that blessed *all* again brought peace and rest to my soul; and though I mourned my sinful backslidings, yet I adored my Saviour who bore *all* my sins.

Hector had a wonderful gift of reading a book and picking out the important points. Sometimes, when staying with him, I would take a book that I had just read; he would take it to bed with him, and the next morning was ready to discuss the most relevant parts. I found these discussions very stimulating, challenging, and sometimes humbling. It was one of my great blessings and joys to be able to relax in this lovely atmosphere, especially when the pastoral charge and preaching had become heavy going. I recall him noting different styles of writing and commenting on how, turning to Professor John Murray on Romans, after reading Lloyd-Jones, was like taking up a nice dry wine. He admired the way Murray never seemed to use an unnecessary word and always seemed to have the best word to convey his meaning.

His catholicity of spirit was also apparent in his reading. He loved the seven volumes of *Wesley's Veterans* so much that he once wrote to me, 'I am reading them very slowly as they must last me the rest of my life, and I do not know how long I may live.' He believed we had much to learn from such men. After reading an article on some much used servants of Christ in the Scottish Highlands whose communion with God gave them such influence with men, he wrote to me:

This is no different from the experience of all John Wesley's Veterans. I have been drawing attention to this for years. We have, in the main, repudiated or disregarded these experiences . . . So great was the overwhelming majesty revealed to them of the holiness of God, and of His great love in forgiving their sins at such a cost, that for a time some of them dwelt in a different world. Their white-hot devotion to Christ, and love and compassion for their fellow creatures, came out of such a revelation. They received power from on high and the Gospel they preached was attended with great blessings. Without such experience Wesley did not encourage them to preach . . . It was not correct doctrine that made them useful: they were often, even generally, unbalanced in this and incorrect, but they had the almost terrifying experience of the Spirit's power in the revelation of a crucified Christ and of what it means to be a perishing sinner. You know me well enough (I hope) to know I do not decry correct doctrine. I strongly believe that evangelicalism has suffered certainly as a result of Arminianism and 'deformed theology' (to use a *Reformation Today* title), neither do I decry long articles on the eldership – even though I am hardly with it – but do not let us get the idea that we must tidy up nicely before God can work. When has He ever waited for that? 'Oh that thou wouldest rend the heavens, that thou wouldest come down.' Please do not think I am criticising Erroll Hulse or *Reformation Today* as they are high on my list of favourites.

In similar vein he wrote to me on another occasion:

I sometimes wonder if I have been placed in this sterile ground of Bathford partly to teach me just this: my longing is to shed much of those inhibitions that tend to separate me from fellow Christians and pursue after Christ alone. He alone is my glorious objective, for the nearer I can get to Him, the greater will be my love to Him, and to all; so greater would be my zeal, and my capacity to serve Him. He is the Ultimate, and to have Him experimentally is to have all, for all blessings come from Him. Then His service would be my delight, and I should walk in measure with the lustre of His glory upon me. Then I should see results from my feeble labours, and not have to mourn my utter barrenness before Him.

There was indeed already more of that 'lustre of His glory' upon our dear friend than he knew.

His death came suddenly on the morning of 28 November 1977. My heart was saddened when I heard the news, for the acute loss to his dear wife, and my own sense of what he had been to me, and that I would no longer enjoy his friendship and company, not least his regular letters. But for him it was joy unspeakable.

The funeral was held in the little chapel at Bathford where he had laboured so hard to maintain a faithful witness and prayed for a season of revival. His dear friend, Iain Murray, conducted the service and preached a beautiful sermon from, 'For to me to live is Christ, and to die is gain.' How true this was for Hector, who could often say, 'My heart leaps at the sound of His name.' A sense of peace pervaded the service and it seemed fitting to come out into the pale December sunshine to walk the short distance to the churchyard where his precious dust was laid to await the glorious resurrection morning.

Sleep on beloved, sleep on and take thy rest,
Lay down thy head upon thy Saviour's breast.
We loved thee well, but Jesus loves thee best.

10

The New Pastorate at Tenterden

I mmediately after my resignation from Jireh there were those who said that I was their pastor and that they wished to sit under my ministry. I advised that we all attend Jireh the following Sunday morning, when a sermon was read, but those supporting me did not return in the afternoon. I rested, as I was due to preach in Canterbury in the evening; quite a number from Jireh attended that service. We at once began to make enquiries as to where we could meet on the following Sunday. These enquiries resulted in our obtaining the Scout Hut, a small wooden building in the centre of the town; the charge was 10s. (50p) for the day, including lighting and heating.

I will never forget that first Sunday morning. I had no idea how many would actually follow me and how many would stay in the old church when it came to making a decision. I used the little kitchen in the Scout Hut as a vestry. The building seated about forty and when I went in on that morning, it was full. Just about half the congregation had come with me. We left with no funds but the people felt that I should not receive less than I had been paid at Jireh and, despite the congregation being halved, the offerings were more than they had been at Jireh. We continued thus for about two years, holding our prayer meetings in our own home. The Lord was very gracious to us, and we had sweet times of fellowship and His presence in our worship. There was often a spirit of wrestling at our prayer meetings.

Soon after our separation, a friend telephoned me to say that he and his wife would give £5,000 towards another building, which in 1967 was a considerable sum. I was about to leave on a short preaching tour. He said that much depended on me and my staying with them. I felt the burden and responsibility of that hour. When I put the receiver down, words that had been impressed upon me before I entered the ministry came with power to my mind: 'Certainly, I will be with thee'. I just wept before the Lord and said, 'Lord, if you will fulfil that, I can ask for nothing more'.

There was a very suitable building in the centre of the town which had been built for the Free Church of England in 1928 by a group that seceded from the national church. No worship had been held there since 1948. Thereafter it was rented to the Kent County Council as a school canteen, but they were about to relinquish it as they had built other accommodation. Our application to them to use it on Sundays met with no success.

In the September following, I had a very bad car accident. I was on my way to preach at Uffington in Berkshire when, in bad conditions, my car skidded across the road and ran head-on into an oncoming car. I opened the door and fell out on to the verge with a broken knee-cap and head injuries. I lay for about half-an-hour when a doctor came, and I heard him say, 'He's in pretty poor shape'. I think they believed me to be unconscious. I was taken to the Radcliffe Infirmary in Oxford, where I remained for ten days. Although I had my leg in plaster for six weeks, I only missed preaching for seven days. I believe the Lord used this accident in two ways. Firstly, it gave me an experience I had never had before. As I was waiting to go into the operating theatre, and as I felt I could be facing death, I knew a sweet assurance that if it was God's will, I could die on the truths I had preached for some years; this gave me a confidence in preaching that I had not had before. Secondly, it brought home to my congregation the difficult situation they would be in if God took me. I believe this further united us as pastor and people; much love and concern was shown, although I think there may have been a few who thought it was a judgment on me.

We drew up new Articles and Rules and called ourselves 'Trinity Baptist Church' (restricted communion), Tenterden. I asked my late friend, Stanley Delves, to approve them. This he did, but on returning them said, 'I am nearly sick of articles of faith; my advice to you is to have as few as possible and minister in love'. Surely, very sound advice, for as the hymnwriter puts it:

> We do all things in vain
> Unless we do all things in love.

We held a service for the formation of the church at Tilden Chapel, Smarden, the mother church of the Strict Baptist churches in Kent. My brethren in the ministry, Robert Oliver of Cheltenham and Harold Crowter were engaged. Pastor Crowter was unable to come, so Pastor David Obbard of Tunbridge Wells took his place. This service was held on 1 September 1967. After the opening hymns, reading and prayer, I read the Covenants and gave brief remarks on the Articles and Rules. David Obbard then gave the right hand of fellowship to me and five members, followed by Robert Oliver doing the same to John Mercer and five members. Mr Obbard then pronounced the twelve members as constituting a gospel church of Jesus Christ to be known as 'Trinity Baptist Church', Tenterden, and offered prayer for the newly formed church. After another hymn was sung, an address was given by David Obbard on the pastoral office (*1 Pet.* 5:2) and Robert Oliver gave the charge to the church (*Rev.* 3:7–13). The communion service followed, a sacred occasion, when about forty participated, some from other churches. We had not advertised this service in any way, but about eighty were present.

A few months after this there was an application by a married couple for baptism and membership. They were unanimously accepted and baptised (again at Tilden Smarden) on 2 March 1968, so the Lord began to add to the church and has continued to do so to this day (1994) when the membership stands at fifty and the congregation at about eighty to ninety.

An application was made to the Free Church of England to use the building, which was soon to be vacated by the Kent County Council, but this was refused. In the summer of 1968, they put the building up to let but did not inform us. I contacted the agents, asking for particulars, and said that we were prepared to meet them. They telephoned me back saying, 'You have been in contact with these Free Church of England people'. When I affirmed this they said, 'They say they are prepared to negotiate with you'.

But still we could make no progress with the authorities concerned for they were willing for anybody to have it to use for any purpose, rather than us, who wanted to use it for the very purpose for which it had been built. In October, we held a special prayer meeting to seek God's aid. One friend, who was visiting, did not pray that God would give it to us, but thanked Him for doing so! I did not feel it was presumptuous as I had never doubted in my mind that God would do this for us. Often, as I drove past that building, especially at night, and saw its dilapidated condition, a prayer would ascend that we might soon restore it for His glory.

The following April (1969) we had a letter saying that it was the unanimous decision of the council of the Free Church of England to let the building to us. We obtained the keys and a few of us were able to inspect it for the first time. Our hearts were filled with joy and thankfulness, and we offered the first prayer within those walls since 1948. They agreed to let it to us on a seven-year lease, with option to renew, the rent being £150 per annum for the first three years and £200 for the last four years. We were to repair and maintain it, and were still renting it when I resigned from the pastorate in 1984.

The building was in a poor state of repair, particularly the decoration. You could hardly drive into the grounds without touching the undercarriage of your car and there were high cypress trees which brushed the roof. We lost no time in starting the renovation work. An application to the town council for permission to remove the trees was granted.

Within the building the roof could scarcely be seen for cobwebs. A caretaker told me that he had only been employed for two hours each week to keep the place clean, so he used to hose down the walls which were of asbestos! Friends did all they could to help and it soon began to take shape. The exterior was a dirty brown pebble dash. This we treated with a white masonry paint which made the building look totally different. The inside walls had to be scrubbed with wire brushes using the strongest detergent possible and took hours of labour. The Lord provided for us in most remarkable ways. An article had appeared in the local press, and one morning when I was working there, a builder pulled up and asked if we needed a pulpit for our church. When I said, 'Yes', he replied, 'I took one out of a chapel some years ago; it was too good to burn so it is still in my workshop'. I went to look at it and could see it was suitable. He said that if I came to help him load it, he would deliver it. It was in three parts and when we re-assembled it on what had been the altar area, you would have thought it had been specially made; it was the same wood and carving as the panelling around the area. This friendly builder also came along when I was laying the tarmac on the drive and said he would send his mechanical roller to roll it in.

The pews were given to us by a large congregational church in Maidstone which had closed. We were able to cut the centre pews in two and remake them from the ends of the side pews. They also gave us a communion table and two chairs, which a friend sent his lorry to collect. One member made all the velvet curtains and the drop for the pulpit book rest.

The opening services were held on Saturday 9 August 1969. The Homewood School allowed us to use their adjoining recreation ground (long since built on) and their facilities, so we erected a marquee which seated about one hundred; this and the church were full for the evening service with some thirty to forty sitting on the grass around.

The weather was beautiful, so some were able to picnic on the grass in addition to the marquee. There was a morning service of prayer and thanksgiving for all the past mercies and to seek God's blessing on the future. The preacher for the afternoon service was Pastor Robert Oliver of Bradford-on-Avon. In the evening service, Pastor Erroll Hulse of Cuckfield and Pastor B. F. Ellis of the Strict Baptist Mission (now the Grace Baptist Mission) were the preachers. Over three hundred gathered that day to hear the glorious gospel; many hearts were blessed and gladdened. The congregation on the following Sundays numbered about seventy, so had nearly doubled since that first gathering on that memorable Sunday in 1967.

The year 1970 was remarkable for two particulars. Early in that year, there were two or three prayer meetings where I believe there was hardly a dry eye; the Lord really seemed to pour a spirit of wrestling prayer upon us and we were sweetly united. That year, we had eight additions to the church. For a church with only fourteen members, that was a touch of revival. After about two years I resumed my systematic preaching in the book of Acts, continuing from where I had left off the last Sunday at Jireh and I believe the Lord graciously owned and blessed those sermons.

The Sunday school had grown to sixty to seventy children and we urgently needed more accommodation, so it was proposed that we erect a hall behind the present building. Application to the town council was made and granted. Application to the Free Church of England to erect a hall as a tenant's fixture was also granted. The hall was erected the following year at a cost of about £1,600.

There were additions to the church almost every year. Our first loss was one of our esteemed deacons, Jesse

Mercer, in November 1970. As some went home to glory, and others had to move elsewhere, others came, and so the church slowly increased and the congregations were maintained.

In 1972 we applied to the Free Church of England to add a covered way from the hall to the back of the church, as children attending the day nursery school had to run out in all weathers to go to the toilets. They agreed to us erecting it (at our own expense) but said they would double the rent! We did not proceed, but added a porch to the hall without consulting them. About this time we were concerned to add a baptistry so that we would not have to use another church on such occasions. The baptistry was duly built and was first used on 23 May 1973.

There were three or four who ultimately returned to Jireh. With hindsight, I believe I can see why they first came with us; I believe they came out of sympathy rather than conviction. We opened a building fund very early on, but as we did not have to purchase the building, the £5,000 was made into a covenant, so finally yielded about £8,000. By the time we were able to purchase (after my retirement), it had grown to about £15,000.

One of my encouragements in these years came from the various conferences which were taking place around the country. Two for pastors, which I endeavoured not to miss, were the Leicester Ministers' Conference (organised by the Banner of Truth Trust) and the Carey Conference. The former began in 1962 and I believe I have attended every year since the mid-1960s. At that time John Murray and W. J. Grier were joint chairmen. Professor Murray was one of the most able theologians of this century; he appeared rather a dour Scot but had a heart of gold. With a marvellous command of language, he never used an unnecessary word but always the best. He was extremely fair and would never give a 'snap' answer. If he was not sure, he would say, 'I will answer that tomorrow morning'. When he preached the closing conference sermon, he could be very simple and often moving, especially if his subject related directly to the Lord Jesus Christ.

W. J. Grier was quite different, not the theologian to the extent that John Murray was, but extremely well read and a very good chairman. I believe he excelled in his judgment of books; for years he had a Christian bookshop in Belfast and would often recommend books that would prove particularly useful to us as ministers. Some of his sermons at the conferences left a lasting impression upon us. The conference owed a great deal to these dear men of God in the early days.

The Carey conference began in January 1970, I being one of the promoters. On that first occasion we met at Waddington, Bromsgrove and the cost for two days was £5.50. This conference came into being as the result of a number of men of Baptist persuasion feeling we needed a conference where we could expand and discuss Baptist principles, which we could not do at the Banner conference. I believe there has never been any opposition between the two conferences, but they have been complementary, each serving its own constituency. I believe the Banner of Truth conference has usually been more devotional while the Carey on the other hand has handled and discussed some difficult subjects affecting our churches. I, for one, have attended all the Carey conferences except two, which were held in the north of England in January.

In 1975 I asked Dr Lloyd-Jones if he could come and preach at our anniversary services at Trinity, Tenterden, and it was arranged that he would come on a July Saturday in 1976. It was a very hot summer but, when I met him at Headcorn station (eight miles from Tenterden), he came off the platform with his overcoat on, a light mac on top and his Homburg hat. The first thing he said was, 'I never get caught in the rain'. I said, 'It has been dry here for weeks'. He replied that there had been a little shower on the way down! I think he enjoyed being with us. He said on his return to the station that the only tune he did not know was the first one. It was called 'Indulgence', composed by a present-day composer. The hymn to which we sang it was one of John Kent's, beginning:

> *Indulgent God! How kind*
> *Are all thy ways to me,*
> *Whose dark, benighted mind*
> *Was enmity to Thee!*
> *Yet now subdued by sov'reign grace*
> *My spirit longs for Thine embrace.*

I had asked if he would stay and preach on Sunday, but he said that when he preached twice on Saturday, he did not now preach on Sunday. The last thing he said to me when he said goodbye at the station was, 'I shall be praying for you tomorrow'. His loving concern touched me deeply. He really did have a heart of gold!

The last occasion the dear Doctor attended the fellowship was, I believe, the first Monday in June 1980. This was the last time I saw him, and I will never forget the opening. Josef Tson of Romania was present, and before the proceedings started, they stood together at the front. Josef, a fine, tall man in his full vigour, the Doctor old and obviously very frail. He said to Josef, 'It is eight years since you were here, and I want to assure you, my wife and I have prayed for you every day during those years'. (Tson had attended the Westminster Fellowship when studying in England). There were tears in Josef's eyes. To me, although I did not realise it at the time, that was a beautiful farewell. Dr Lloyd-Jones was supremely a man of prayer. The prayer that he offered at the close of the meetings that day was truly blessed and uplifting, and I believe many felt it to be so. He died on 1 March 1981.

Over the years, we had our share of problems as all churches do. There are no problems in a cemetery, but have a house full of children and you will surely have some. Yet nothing broke the fellowship. At one period I was conscious of some discontent with the ministry, so I proposed to the deacons that we should call a special church meeting at which the members would be free to say exactly what they felt, and be assured that I would take no offence. At this meeting there were criticisms and appreciations. One young member said, 'We had Mr So and So, and I thought he was fantastic'. I replied, 'I am sure he was fantastic, but if he came every Sunday, he would be less fantastic'. The discussion did a great deal of good; it cleared the air and the same spirit was never again manifest. As pastors we may often fail, but it seems to me that we should be honest with one another.

When I was sixty-nine years of age, a young member visited me and suggested that it might be time I thought about retiring. I must admit that as I was still in excellent health and things seemed satisfactory at the church, I had no thoughts of that kind. But it led me to give serious thought to the subject. I did not want to become a hindrance to the work. When I reached my seventieth birthday, I felt it was right to give them two years' notice of retirement, but stated that if they called someone before that time, I would be willing to stand down. This I did three months before the two years expired to allow Peter Sanderson of Sheffield to accept the pastorate. My last official duty was to receive him and his wife and son into membership.

The induction service for the new pastor was held on Saturday 15 September 1984 when the church was full. Pastor Leslie Jarvis gave the charge to the church and Pastor John Turner, the charge to the pastor. I was asked to take the main prayer. Of course, I knew mixed feelings in doing so, but I sincerely desired that God would richly bless his ministry. One Sunday, two or three years before I retired, I was in earnest prayer in my study, and I believe God gave me faith to say, 'Lord, if you will hear my prayer for blessing and increase, grant that there may be one fresh person in the congregation this morning'. For some reason we were holding the services in the hall that day, and when I went in early to check things, there sat a person whom I had never seen before and have never seen since. God has answered my prayer, for He has doubled the congregation since that day.

On Saturday 24 November 1984, a service of thanksgiving for God's mercy during the twenty-four years of ministry in Tenterden was held to mark my retirement. The church was well filled. John McDonald (an elder) presided and during the service presented me with an elm garden seat on behalf of the church and congregation. Norman Hopkins (an elder) gave a review of the history of Trinity, paying a tribute to my labours. My dear friend, Dr Robert Oliver, preached a moving sermon. It was again a time of mixed feelings for me and I felt humbled and thankful for God's great goodness over many years. I chose the closing hymn:

> *Jerusalem, my happy home,*
> *Name ever dear to me!*
> *When shall my labours have an end,*
> *In joy and peace and Thee?*

Tea was served afterwards. My wife was in hospital, so was unable to attend.

Thus another chapter in my life closed, reminding me that the greater part lies in the past. I desire to be prepared for what might still lie before me and for that call which must come to all, which all will have to obey.

> *Prepare me, gracious God,*
> *To stand before Thy face,*
> *Thy Spirit must the work perform,*
> *For it is all of grace.*

II

Retirement – Calmer Waters

For years I had said that pastors should not continue when their powers are failing. I had known several who had held pastorates for over fifty years and who, I felt, had unwittingly become dictators. Generations had grown up under them and their word almost became law. When they were taken home, the churches were often unfitted to carry on, no provision having been made for another man to take the oversight. Having advanced this conviction, it was only right that I should practise what I preached.

Another cause why some men continued too long was that no financial provision was made for their retirement. I felt that if it was right for me to retire, the Lord would make provision for me. I was quite willing to find some employment to augment my income, and have cared for several small gardens whose owners were no longer able to do so. I was still able to do a fair amount of preaching. One of the unlooked-for ways in which God provided for us was through the Particular Baptist Fund. Years ago, a legacy was left to provide eleven men with an annual grant for distinguished service in the denomination. A vacancy had just occurred, and they allocated it to me, sending me a cheque. I would never need to apply and would receive it for the remainder of my life. The amount has increased most years. We also sold our large house and purchased a smaller one, which gave us £9,000 to invest. Thus far our needs have been supplied.

I believe it is very important that as we grow older, we have plenty of interests. It seems to me to be fatal to put your feet up! My great interest apart from the Lord's work has been gardening. I am certain that the Lord provided this house and garden for us. We were two years selling our former home and had made offers on three others; finally when we had a buyer, the house we were hoping to buy was sold. In my daily reading that morning in October 1983, I read II Chronicles 29:36, 'Hezekiah and all the people rejoiced at what God had brought about for His people, because it was done quickly'. We made an offer for another property which had seemed suitable, and there were just three days between signing the contracts and moving in! When I walked into the garden I could see that it had real possibilities. It was sheltered and faced south, but contained little but weeds and rough grass. After clearing, I began to landscape it, having a picture in my mind. Being a small garden (less than one quarter acre) I did two things. First of all I covered all the fences with climbers and shrubs, which at once gives the impression of greater size, as it merges into the surroundings. Then I made as many vistas as possible. I now have about eight, with focal points containing a statue or seat. Having clothed the boundary one has been able to include many plants to create a subtropical atmosphere, using such plants as palms and tree ferns, climbing roses combined with clematis – one of my favourite climbers, of which I now have about 120 varieties, some raised from my own seed. Then below these are many varieties of bulbs, about 50 varieties of hardy ferns (now becoming as popular as they were in Victorian days) and a wide variety of herbaceous plants. I believe the garden now contains one of the largest collections of plants for a small garden in the south east of England. The other attraction is a large number of containers, filled in summer with quite exotic plants, which are arranged mainly on the large patio which we built.

For seven years the garden has been open to the public on certain days. We also entertain parties from various parts of the world, including the U.S.A. and Australia. People from the European continent are constant visitors; one young couple actually drove from Belgium and back in a day to see the garden! Our visitors book which contains hundreds of signatures, is witness to the delight and appreciation of many. We open under the National Garden Scheme, receiving seven to eight hundred visitors yearly, and have raised several thousands of pounds for charity. This gives pleasure to us and to many others and we meet many interesting folk.

I believe that provided we do not make idols of God's gifts, we may enjoy them. 'He giveth us all things richly to enjoy'. I believe it is significant that God placed our first parents in a garden and I look forward to 'the new heavens and new earth wherein dwelleth righteousness'. What must it be to be there?

It is not easy to stand down after holding the pastoral office for nearly a quarter of a century, but I determined not to interfere, and to give the new pastor my support. It seemed to me that as I had tried to be a good pastor, so now I should prove myself to be a good member. I allowed no-one to come to me and I stopped visiting, except for two or three old members, with the new pastor's approval. My mother often prayed that she might grow old graciously and that is my desire. As those with long experience, I believe we can give some advice and help to our younger brethren. I still serve on a number of committees and go regularly to several ministers' fraternals. It would be easy to give them up, but I believe attendance to be useful. We need to keep in touch with the events and trends in the churches.

I have gone to my successor on a very few occasions when there was something I was not quite happy with. I have never spoken behind his back. In some cases it may be better for a retiring pastor to go somewhere else, but I had no desire or leadings to do that.

I wish to pay tribute to my wife, Gwendoline. From my entry into the ministry, she has never put anything in my way in carrying out my preaching engagements or my pastoral office. Particularly when our children, David and Peter, were young, this laid a heavy task upon her. The churches which we served did not appreciate that a pastor needed a rest day as well as others. We had no financial reserves and often had to wait upon God to supply our needs, which He did in various ways. When we first came to Tenterden in 1961 we were paid £8 per week; we had to meet all our expenses except our rates which the church paid, obtaining 50% reduction on the manse.

My late friend, George Rose, once said to me, 'If you put God's work first, He will see to it that you never lack' – and so it proved. To a lady who once said to him that she believed the Lord had given her the promise, 'Thy bread shall be given thee, and thy water shall be sure,' he said,

'That does not mean you are going to live in affluence!'

I have continued to attend the Westminster Fellowship. The monthly attendance is now small compared with former days, but we profit from our discussions under the leadership of our two chairmen, Hywel Jones and Graham Harrison. It is a long day as we have a morning and afternoon session, and I have a business meeting in the evening. I look on that as a day's work. I also usually attend the monthly flower show of the Royal Horticultural Society, also held at Westminster; that is my day out!

The sense of debt which I owe to Spurgeon abides and it meant much to me that exactly one hundred years after his death, I stood with my dear elder son, at his grave in South London. A little while before I had said to my son, 'I want you to take me to Norwood Cemetery on 31 January 1992', and he kindly complied. At the spot we re-read the address given by Archibald Brown on that occasion. It was a time of deep reflection for me and of earnest prayer as we thought of the future.

My preaching engagements are growing fewer, but when the Lord graciously endues and we can preach the glorious gospel and extol a precious Christ, it is still the greatest joy in this life, and to know that at times God has used us to bless needy souls is indeed a great honour and should deeply humble us. How blessed to have spiritual children and one day hear the wonderful sentence from our Lord and Master, 'Well done, good and faithful servant, enter thou into the joy of thy Lord.'

In my latter years I want to sum up the situation as I see things. In looking back over my eighty years, regarding the church in this land I believe we have seen a deep trough, reaching rock bottom about 1940 when the spiritual life was surely at a very low ebb. Although the condition of our country generally is even worse than in 1940 I believe there have been many encouraging signs. Beginning with the pulpit, the men I knew earlier this century had little vision as to the church's future. That is very different with the younger men today, many of whom do believe in a time of blessing yet to come. There are certainly many more men faithfully preaching the gospel. I believe in many instances the standard of the ministry is higher, with sound exposition and practical application combined with experience.

Many new churches are coming into being, in some areas where, for years, there has been no faithful witness. Many of these fellowships want to be governed by Scripture alone and are autonomous, which I believe is the New Testament pattern with fellowship between like-minded churches.

Conferences and fraternals are playing their part. When I first attended the Banner of Truth conference thirty years ago there were about forty men attending, now it is around four hundred. The same applies to some other Christian conferences, including Carey. This is most encouraging. Another feature of the last decade is the number of men from overseas who join with us and can testify to God's blessing in their respective countries.

Then, literature and radio are playing a very important part with sound and challenging books being widely circulated, so that today there is no dearth of good books in the English language on every aspect of the church and of the Christian life. The Bible teaches us we should not remain children in knowledge but grow up into maturity. Certainly churches need such members to be able to bear an effectual witness to the world.

I believe two things are needed, which God has joined together as we read in Ezekiel 36:37, 38. The church needs to be on her knees in earnest agonising prayer for God to return in power to revive and build; then for the Lord to pour out graciously His Spirit in mighty power and we shall behold, 'the Glory of the knowledge of the Lord, shall cover the earth as the waters cover the seas.' I close this little account of my pilgrimage with an earnest plea to all our young people in particular so to plead with our gracious God that they may see such a glorious time, when I am under a coverlet of grass.

Index